COLLECTING SCIENCE FICTION AND FANTASY

GARY LOVISI

Alliance Publishing, Inc.

*-To Bill Lyles and Paul Payne,
two great guys, good friends,
and pioneer collectors and scholars.*

Copyright © 1997
by Gary Lovisi
All rights reserved.
No portion of this book may be reproduced in any form
without written permission from the publisher.

ISBN 1-887110-12-7

Design by Cynthia Dunne

Alliance Books are available at special discounts for bulk
purchases for sales and promotions, premiums, fund
raising, or educational use.
For details, contact:

Alliance Publishing, Inc.
P. O. Box 080377
Brooklyn, New York 11208-0002

Distributed to the trade by National Book Network, Inc.

10 9 8 7 6 5 4 3 2 1

CONTENTS:

Introduction: What Is an Instant Expert? ....*v*

CHAPTER 1:
Getting Started *1*
   The Importance of Cover Art *1*
   15 Top Collectible SF/F/H Paperback
      Cover Artists *4*
   15 Top Collectible SF/F/H/Authors *10*
   How to Budget a Collection *17*

CHAPTER 2:
A Brief History of Collecting
Paperback SF/F/H *21*
   The Pioneer Days of the Horror Paperback .. *24*
   The Pioneer Days of the Fantasy Paperback .. *29*
   The Pioneer Days of the Science
      Fiction Paperback *37*
   SF/F/H in the Later
      Vintage Era: 1952–1970 .... *44*
   The 1970s Science Fiction Boom *52*
   The 1980s Horror Boom *53*
   The 1990s Fantasy Boom *56*
   The Star Trek and Star Wars
      Paperback Boom *58*
   SF/F/H Movie and TV Tie-in Paperbacks .. *62*

CHAPTER 3:
Think and Talk Like an Expert *69*
   The Importance of Condition *69*
   How to Grade a Paperback *74*
   Market Trends *76*
   Basic Vocabulary and Glossary *80*
   The Want List *84*

You Have to Be Able to Walk Away *85*
Best Condition is Always Best *86*
Networking *86*
How to Tell Reprints *87*
Dealers' Lists: a Good Place to Buy *89*
Foreign Editions *90*

CHAPTER 4:
All About Paperbacks *93*
How and Why Paperback Collecting Began ..*93*
The Non-Collector Collector *96*
50 Most Valuable SF/F/H Paperbacks at Auction *97*
20 Collectible SF/F/H Publisher Imprints and Series *104*
20 SF/F/H Authors and Their Pseudonyms .*112*

CHAPTER 5:
Collector's Guide *117*
Reference Material *117*
Directory of Specialist Paperback Dealers ...*120*
Paperback Shows and Conventions *123*
Paperback Auctions and Auction Houses *125*
How to Sell Your Collection *127*
Becoming a Dealer *128*
Selling to a Dealer *128*

CHAPTER 6:
Instant Expert Quiz *131*

About the Author *133*
Index *135*

INTRODUCTION

WHAT IS AN INSTANT EXPERT?

Science Fiction, Fantasy, and Horror are the modern literary genres of imagination and ideas. These books, especially the mass-market paperbacks, are increasingly prized today by readers and collectors worldwide because of the universality and importance of their authors' visions. They are also collected because of the art on the covers and the artists who created it. These are the books (many of them now classics) that an entire generation of Baby Boomers read when they were growing up. Their children now read them in various reprints of those earlier, original paperback editions published in the 50s and 60s.

This book was written with the goal of serving as a guide for the reader, fan, book lover, and collector of science fiction, fantasy, and horror in paperback form. Paperback publication is where almost all of this work has traditionally appeared, and out of which these genres eventually grew and matured to become the dominant and lucrative publishing categories they are today.

Most of all, I have tried to make this book fun and informative to enable you to become an Instant Expert in this field, whether you are a fan, collector, or book dealer. I've tried to share my enthusiasm as a fan and collector of these books for over 25 years. Collecting this material is a wonderful hobby, and this book, *Instant Expert: Collecting Science Fiction, Fantasy, and Horror in Paperback*, can help you avoid many of the pitfalls and mistakes too many novice collectors often make. At the same time, the book offers valuable tips, firsthand experience, and quite a bit of book chat (book collectors do, after all, love to talk *about books*) that, I'm sure, many SF/F/H fans and collectors and general book collectors will enjoy. The many cover reproductions throughout the book offer the reader the opportunity to see some of the most collectible and key books in the SF/F/H genres. These are prized or influential books not often seen these days.

This book is devoted almost exclusively to paperback books for a variety of reasons. Paperbacks were long neglected by book collectors because of an unfortunate elitist attitude by many in the book field that has finally been breached by common sense. It is also unfortunate that that attitude caused many collectors and dealers to miss the boat on some exceptionally desirable, collectible, and valuable books. The SF/F/H genres have been primarily paperback genres, with books often having original publication in paperback (as PBO's, paperback originals). These books were read and collected by fans as paperback collectibles. Softcover books originally were a manifestation of our disposable culture, printed to be read and then thrown out, without any permanence whatsoever. Nevertheless, many people kept the books they loved to read, some to read them again and again, others because of the wonderful covers. The books were just so attractive. And so, paperback collecting was born.

It all comes full circle: Today many of these same paperback originals from years ago are reprinted in paperback and often in hardcover. However, it is the original paperback editions that are the true first editions and worth good money today.

Lastly, while plenty of books have been written about SF/F/H, they all take the perspective of the mainstream or hardcover publishers regarding the actual books themselves as collectible items. There is a large part of this story that has, until this book, been left out of most SF/F/H histories. The paperback story in SF/F/H! It's important and fascinating. The popularity of these three genres, their authors, and their artists primarily comes from the mass-market *paperback* editions, so paperback publishers and the books they published are key to understanding the genres, the authors, artists, and the works themselves. Paperback publishing in these genres has had a long and somewhat checkered history, but at least it has been interesting. I'll try to incorporate some of that history where it concerns subjects I've covered or collectible editions that I talk about in the text.

The SF/F/H paperback story has never really been told before, and this book is the only one to seriously examine the topic. This book is full of much new and in some cases never-before-published information. It was written to be of value to and for the enjoyment of the SF/F/H fan and collector, the novice entering the collecting hobby, experienced old hands, and even dealers and book scouts.

Paperbacks are fun and paperback collecting is a wonderful hobby. Enjoy it. You too can become an Instant Expert with the help of this book.

GETTING STARTED

CHAPTER 1

THE IMPORTANCE OF COVER ART

Perhaps the most important aspect of a collectible science fiction, fantasy, or horror paperback, other than the overall condition of the book itself (which I cover elsewhere), is the cover art and the cover artist.

Each cover artist for books in these three genres of imaginative literature has to deal with a very special set of parameters. His other job is to interpret a particular work of fiction in an illustrative form that must be compelling enough to ensure attention from the book-buying public and eventually ensure the purchase of that book by the public. *You*, the reader. In other words, the cover image must be striking and make the prospective reader want to buy the book.

Cover artists for imaginative literature have one other challenge that so-called mainstream, realistic, or bestseller fiction (in the general term of that phrase) artists do not have. Cover art for books of imaginative fiction must depict things that do not exist, in many cases have never existed, and in all probability may never exist. In the hands of a truly talented artist these covers can show the best in imaginative art, truly stunning and breathtaking work. It's

1

INSTANT EXPERT

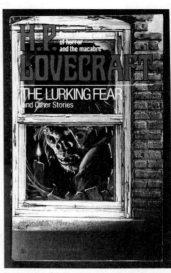

The Lurking Fear *by H.P. Lovecraft (Del Rey Books, 1980s), with incredible Michael Whelan cover.*

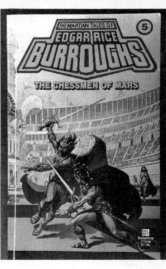

The Chessmen of Mars *by Edgar Rice Burroughs (Del Rey Books #27838, 1980s), classic Mars novel with stunning Michael Whelan cover art.*

exciting. It's fantastic. It is art that mixes the commercial attention-getting aspects of illustration, to make a sale, with the best aspects of design, innovation, and true artistic talent. There can be few guidelines in this area, and the better artists (those with long track records, talented masters who are collected avidly) sometimes are given carte blanche by publishers, editors, and art directors to stamp their own unique interpretation of the work into the cover for the book.

Some recent examples of a master artist given freedom to interpret a famous author's classic work are the wonderful and chilling Michael Whelan covers done for the H.P. Lovecraft Ballantine paperback reprint series of this famous author's horror novels. Whelan also did a special series of covers for Edgar Rice Burroughs' famed Martian SF novels. Combining fantasy with SF, Whelan also did a magnificent group of covers for the dragon novels in Anne McCaffrey's Pern series. These are just a few choice examples from only one artist's work.

In many cases the artist must create images and moods, characters and heroes out of whole cloth, or painstakingly and carefully extract them from the written work itself. It's a challenge and a lot of hard work for cover artists, but it's also a liberating experience for them to be able to delve into new and unknown worlds and to interpret these worlds for millions of readers. Many of these artists are also big fans of the work they illustrate, which comes

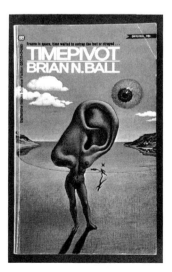

Timepivot *by Brian N. Ball (Ballantine Books, 1970s), Dali-esque cover art gives more surreal and serious image to SF.*

through in their work. Michael Whelan is certainly a fan of Edgar Rice Burroughs' Martian novels and of the horror work of H.P. Lovecraft. His love of these works and respect for them shows in his cover art for these books. He's not only a fabulously talented artist, he's also a fan of the writers whose work he illustrates. That is important. And Whelan is not alone in this regard. The best cover artists, the ones avidly collected, the ones who can sell a book just because it has a cover by them, are also fans of the work they illustrate. They understand the work, and their art, rather than being merely a sales gimmick with commercial considerations, goes far beyond that aspect. In the best cases it is art that actually enhances the original work. And often it can stand apart from that work as art and be enjoyed for its own sake.

Many of the better artists have done dozens of outstanding covers, if not many hundreds of paperback covers over their careers. Many of these artists also have their own devoted fans, just like authors and like movie stars.

Collecting their work is an enjoyable and enlightening experience and a prime reason why people collect these books in the first place.

15 Top Collectible SF/F/H Paperback Cover Artists

While this list is somewhat subjective, I've tried to list the cover artists who are perennially collected by knowledgeable fans and collectors in the SF/F/H fields. These are artists whose books are bought avidly by collectors *and* noncollectors. Many of these books are purchased for one sole reason, because the book may have cover art by a particular collectible artist on this list. Needless to say, there are also artists whose originals constantly sell at high prices.

Perhaps the truest test of a collectible science fiction, fantasy, or horror paperback artist is this: Will readers buy the book *solely* because it has a cover by that particular artist? That is, will they actually collect the books for the cover art alone, regardless of the contents? Well, it happens, and quite often. Paperbacks with Frank Frazetta covers, Michael Whelan covers, or James Warhola covers are just a few examples of books that sell solely because of the cover art, or the name of the artist. In such cases, the author, even a big-name author, or the genre of the book, may not be that important to the buyer. The artist *is*! And these artists do sell books. There are collectors who will buy *any* book with a Frazetta cover, or a Whelan cover, or any book with many of the master artists on the following list. Let's take a look.

JILL BAUMAN: Her work in the horror and fantasy field is well known and respected by fans and authors alike. She's done incredible covers for Charles Grant's horror novels and anthologies as well as the books of Stephen King, F. Paul Wilson, and many others. Realistic, colorful, and wonderful work.

VINCENT DIFATE: Since the late 1960s DiFate has been doing excellent cover art for science fiction paperbacks and some fantasy novels. His work is realistic, but often with a touch of the surreal.

LEO and DIANE DILLON: A husband and wife team whose modern approach to science fiction illustration has given the genre an adult and serious look that many authors and fans enjoy and admire. Their covers for many of Harlan Ellison's paperbacks are classics of the genre. They are also accomplished children's books illustrators.

ED EMSH: One of the stalwarts of the digest magazines and paperback books of the 50s and 60s. He did many wonderful covers for Ace Books and Lancer Books in the science fiction and fantasy genres. One of the classic illustrators of SF and a massive talent.

KELLY FREAS: Another classic illustrator of the

INSTANT EXPERT

The Spell of Seven, *edited by L. Sprage de Camp (Pyramid Books #R1192, 1969), sword and sorcery collection with a fabulous Virgil Findlay skull cover.*

Martians, Go Home *by Fredric Brown (Ballantine Books #25314, 1970s reprint), great little green men invasion novel, with classic Kelly Freas cover.*

50s (his Astounding covers are legend) who did many fine covers for Ace Books, Lancer's Asimov titles, Daw Books, and the entire Laser Books series. Still alive and an active artist, Freas should be declared a national treasure.

VIRGIL FINDLAY: While primarily a pulp magazine illustrator, he did covers and interiors on the

COLLECTING SCIENCE FICTION AND FANTASY

The 1,000-Year Plan *by Isaac Asimov (Ace Books #D-110, 1950s), retitling of* Foundation *with classic Ed Emsh cover art.*

pulps of the 40s and 50s. Findlay also did a few covers for paperback books (and many for hardcovers). Classic paperback covers include his eerie graveyard scene for the Pyramid edition of *Weird Tales* and the famous red skull cover for *The Spell of Seven*. He makes up in quality for what he lacks in quantity.

FRANK FRAZETTA: There's not much that hasn't been said about Frank Frazetta's work. He's an incredible talent and has done over a hundred paperback cover paintings. They're all wonderful work, full of raw and powerful passion, strong heroes and gorgeous women (Frazetta women are a wonder to behold!), all fighting incredible monsters. Frazetta's Conan covers for Lancer Books and his early cover art on the small Ace Books editions of Edgar Rice Burroughs' novels in the 60s are a treasure. His work is often imitated but never matched or eclipsed. Highly collected, many of his scarcer books sell at good prices.

JEFF JONES: This artist did many fine covers for science fiction, fantasy, and horror books in the 60s and 70s, many for Lancer Books. A very talented artist who used surreal images and mystery to enhance the power of his horror and fantasy art.

DENNIS MCLOUGHLIN: While he did not do much SF or fantasy, this British artist did create a lot of hardboiled crime and humor art. He also did much comic book work (some of it SF). A very talented and collectible artist but not as well known here as he should be.

HARRY O. MORRIS: His computer-created and photo-collage covers for magazines and books, such as those in the Dell Abyss horror line, are classic horror covers. A very talented and hardworking artist who brings much innovation to the genre.

RICHARD POWERS: A stalwart of the 50s and 60s, he was brought on the SF scene by Ian Ballantine to do covers for many of the Ballantine science fiction novels. His work is very surreal and gave the genre an adult and serious look that it greatly needed at a time when pulp-inspired work was keeping the genre in a literary ghetto. Powers did hundreds of excellent covers, and was often imitated.

H.R. VAN DONGEN: From his 50s Astounding SF covers, this artist came back and became a stalwart of cover illustration for Ballantine Books in the 1970s and 1980s. A unique talent whose images can appear so alien and so everyday, they form a nice combination, offering thoughtful (and sometimes humorous) and insightful SF art. A very underrated artist, whose art is also often very understated.

JAMES WARHOLA: Warhola mixes humor into his cover illustrations, bright with wild colors, fascinating images, and probably the greatest aliens outside of Barclay Shaw's. Warhola covers offer a special treat; they are full of wonder and are great fun. He's a very popular artist, and justly so.

MICHAEL WHELAN: One of the kings of realistic illustration, Whelan is a stunningly talented artist and has done covers for many of the best and biggest names in the SF/F/H genres. His work is always a joy to behold, and paperbacks with his covers are avidly collected.

RON TURNER: Another British artist who did much of his work on science fiction books in the 50s in England for the so-called "Mushroom Publishers." Turner mixes great images with wild and bright colors and an exciting illustration technique. He's still active today, doing among other things, SF and crime covers for my own Gryphon Publications. A very underrated artist and relatively unknown here, but one of the true greats.

HONORABLE MENTION: While masters such as J.K. Potter and H.R. Giger are incredibly talented and highly collected, their work mainly appears on hardcover books or magazines, or in other media. In many cases their work is not standard illustration but consists of photos or computer-generated photo work. It's highly effective and collected, but relative to most other artists the number of paperback covers they have done is, unfortunately, few and far between.

Other artists deserving honorable mention (a complete list would be far too long, so I'm sure I've left some people out) are: Roy Krenkel, Laurence Schwinger, Gil Cohen, Kenneth Smith, Don Maitz, Richard Hescox, Jack Gaughan, Stanley Meltzoff (his incredible Signet SF covers in the 50s), James Avati (a master artist, but since he did so little SF, his impact in this book is unfortunately limited), Robert Maguire, Robert McGinnis, Mitchell Hooks, and Walter Popp (all extraordinary artists and highly collected, but their work is primarily in other genres so I've only been able to give them an honorable mention here), Barclay Shaw, Darrell K. Sweet, the Brothers Hildebrandt, Gray Morrow, Paul Lehr, Tim Kirk, Jim Burns, Ken Kelly, Earl Bergey, Jim Steranko, and just so many others.

INSTANT EXPERT

The Caves of Steel by Isaac Asimov (Pyramid Books #F-784, 1960s), classic robot novel.

15 TOP COLLECTIBLE SF/F/H AUTHORS

What makes an author collectible is not always easy to determine. Popularity and high sales certainly matter, sometimes the right cover artist (Frazetta on the Conan books, for instance) can certainly help, but perhaps the best indication is the strength of the author's vision and the quality of the writing. Another important factor is: What does the author's work say? If the themes are timeless, or very important, or new and ground-breaking, then it's a good bet the work will be highly influential and well received. Maybe controversial. Which can be good. Maybe even important. Which is better. Sometimes it can take a combination of these factors.

The following list contains the names of 15 top collectible authors in the genres of science fiction, fantasy, and horror, and a bit about each of them. In some cases the genres overlap, but in all cases the authors are giant figures whose work is perennially popular and collectible.

ISAAC ASIMOV: One of the greatest SF writers and one of the most popular. He wrote the famed Foundation series and the Robot novels. There *will* be an Asimov revival. He was a nice guy, too, a

COLLECTING SCIENCE FICTION AND FANTASY

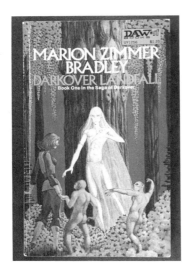

Darkover Landfall *by Marion Zimmer Bradley (DAW Books, 2nd printing), with new cover art, first book in the popular Darkover SF series.*

first-class gentleman and a true genius who popularized science for millions of people.

ROBERT BLOCH: Horror master from the days of *Weird Tales* and H.P. Lovecraft, through the 1960s with *Psycho*, and to the recent era when he was still popular and producing spine-tingling work. Always collectible.

MARION ZIMMER BRADLEY: Humanistic science fiction from a woman's point of view, and also containing feminist views, but overall she is just an excellent storyteller whose earlier Darkover books are wonderful classics. She also wrote in non-SF/F/H genres and under different names in those genres. All her work is collected.

EDGAR RICE BURROUGHS: The creator of Tarzan and John Carter of Mars, and so much more. Immensely popular and highly collected, much of it going for big bucks. One of the greatest natural storytellers of all time.

PHILIP K. DICK: A great imaginative speculative fiction writer, creator of classic books, many of which were PBO's. The films *Total Recall* and *Bladerunner* were made from his works. Highly col-

INSTANT EXPERT

Bladerunner *by Philip K. Dick (Del Rey Books, 1980s), movie tie-in with Dick's original novel.*

The Man in the High Castle *by Philip K. Dick (Popular Library #SP250, 1964), SF novel gets the bestseller treatment.*

lectible, his books have yet to reach their peak in the market.

HARLAN ELLISON: This great "Bad Boy" of science fiction is an imaginative writer of incredible talent, highly popular and highly collected. Always interesting.

ROBERT A. HEINLEIN: Harder science fiction

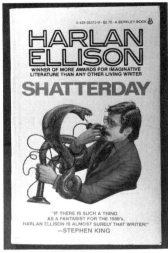

Shatterday *by Harlan Ellison (Berkley Books, 1980s), great collection of his short fiction with the author pictured on the cover.*

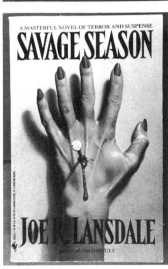

Savage Season *by Joe R. Lansdale (Bantam Books, 1980s), one of his many collectible horror titles.*

with a more right-wing interpretation, great classic fiction, and hardboiled characters. One of SF's greats, very much missed today. A Heinlein revival might also be around the corner in a few years.

ROBERT E. HOWARD: Practically invented the sub-genre of sword and sorcery, the creator of Conan the Barbarian, and the greatest writer

INSTANT EXPERT

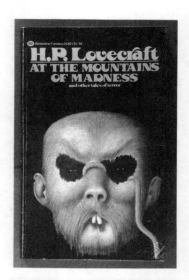

At the Mountains of Madness by H.P. Lovecraft (Ballantine Books, 1970s), Brown Jenkin as portrayed by John Holmes.

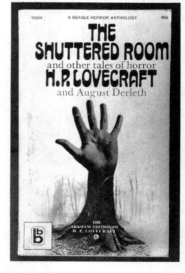

The Shuttered Room by H.P. Lovecraft (Beagle Books #95068), obscure 1970s series of classic horror.

there ever was of what made pulp fiction exciting. Highly collected and more popular than ever.

STEPHEN KING: Modern horror seems to have been founded by, or for, King. He's taken all the various strains of the genre and by giving them a

COLLECTING SCIENCE FICTION AND FANTASY

Hell House
by Richard Matheson (Bantam Books #N7277, 1970s), horror gets the Gothic cover treatment.

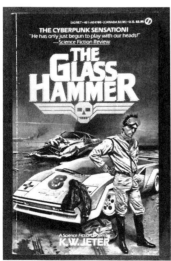

The Glass Hammer
by K.W. Jeter (Signet Books, 1980s), collectible cyberpunk SF novel.

modern interpretation built a one-man fiction factory. Incredibly collected.

DEAN KOONTZ: Another giant in modern horror who came out of the science fiction genre in the 1960s. Highly collected and collectible.

JOE LANSDALE: A tremendously talented writer whose earlier work was primarily horror. Has strong fan appeal and is highly collected. A future superstar.

H.P. LOVECRAFT: Father of the paranoid horror story, and creator of the Cthulthu Mythos, an incredibly popular and highly collected author. A perennial subject of serious scholarly study.

RICHARD MATHESON: A very prolific and versatile author who is at home in science fiction as he is in fantasy and horror (and even westerns). Highly collected and still doing fine work.

MICHAEL MOORCOCK: British author, creator of the excellent Elric sword and sorcery series and much other fine material. An interesting and versatile writer of great talent; highly collectible.

ANDRE NORTON: A rather prolific author whose work has been very influential with women and in the fantasy field. She's very popular and highly collected, and while many of her books do not go for big money yet, I feel her work is a real sleeper in the collectible market.

HONORABLE MENTION: There are so many more great authors in these three genres, and again I'm sure I've barely scratched the surface and left many collectible authors out. But honorable mention should also be said of the following: William F. Nolan, Ron Goulart, E.C. Tubb, Robert McCammon, Dan Simmons, K.W. Jeter, J.N. Williamson, Ray Garton, Tom Disch, Ray Russell, August Derleth, Richard Lupoff, C.J. Cherryh, Janny Wurts, Barbara Paul (her early SF and F), Henry Kuttner, C.L. Moore, Murray Leinster, Damon Knight, Fritz Lieber, J.R.R. Tolkien, Fred Brown (in his SF/F/H mode), L. Sprague deCamp, Poul Anderson, Fred Pohl, C.M. Kornbluth, Orson Scott Card, Robert Asprin, Glen Cook, George Alec Effinger, Peter F. Hamilton, John Russell Fearn, Kirk Mitchell, Clive Barker, Leigh Brackett, Eric

Frank Russell, Alan Dean Foster, Arthur C. Clarke, Gene Wolfe, Ramsey Campbell, Lois McMaster Bujold, Clark Ashton Smith, F. Paul Wilson, Colin Wilson, Roger Zelazny, Guy N. Smith (his U.K. originals), Jack Vance, Sax Rohmer, Kurt Vonnegut, Jr., Philip Jose Farmer, Theodore Sturgeon, Robert Silverberg, Brian Lumley, Manly Wade Wellman, Joanna Russ, Ursula LeGuin, Larry Niven, H. Beam Piper, Dennis Etchison, Anne McCaffrey, Bruce Sterling, William Gibson, Craig Shaw Gardner, James Tiptree, and about a thousand other fine writers who are also very collectible.

How to Budget a Collection

Most collectors are also regular people (in many cases just like you and me, as strange as that may seem at times, especially if you know collectors). They are on a budget just like everyone else. However, it's a good idea for collectors to have a budget for their collecting purchases and to adhere to it. It can be difficult, especially when a collector encounters so many choice items that he or she *must* have.

The best advice I can give someone who finds himself between that rock and a hard place—an avid collector with limited funds to spend on his collection amidst the feeding frenzy of buying *must have* items for it—is to consider his purchases with care and intelligence. That often means, though not always, buying with an eye toward future resale value or an appreciation of value down the road, perhaps when the individual may want to sell that particular item.

One of the best ways to budget yourself is to give yourself a monthly allowance—kind of like when you were a kid. In fact, since many people (usually spouses, but also collectors themselves) often state that collectors are really just a bunch of overgrown kids anyway, an allowance will help you keep your buying under control so that you do not overspend. Overspending in general, or spending too much on a particular item (usually at auction), or just book gluttony (wanting to buy up *everything*) can be a real problem. And you will sometimes come across great deals that will make it even more difficult to pass up some of these items. Auctions, while offering the opportunity to acquire scarce and highly desirable items, can also fuel a feeding frenzy and blow a budget right out of the water. You can spend or buy yourself into a serious cash flow problem here if not careful.

One of the best ways to feed your book collecting habit and maintain and expand your collection with a minimum cash outlay is to trade with fellow collectors. Find collectors in your area and cultivate them. They'll make good friends and companions and will be an added source of fascination by being a good source of news, information, *and* cheap books.

Trade your dupes (duplicate copies) for the dupes of another collector. If you're a science fiction collector and are trading with another science fiction collector, you'll probably both have something each can use from the other's collection. This can save you a lot of money. It's also good to have a collector friend who shares your own interests. It can be the best of all worlds.

You can also trade with collectors who don't share your interests. You'd be surprised what collectors can come up with, and quite often a mystery or western collector may have some very nice SF/F/H to sell or trade. Some great trades can be made this way, great for both parties since each person is getting rid of items he does not want or isn't interested in collecting and is getting things in return that he does want, often at a very good price and sometimes for no money at all. What could be better?

However, even if you don't trade, if you happen to buy books outright from a fellow collector, then you'll still be ahead and will probably be paying a lot less than dealer prices. Usually. The book collecting hobby has operated in just this way for decades, but with key books in the better grades getting scarce, and more people coming into the hobby, the supply of good books (i.e., collectible books) has dwindled and dealers have taken a bigger hand as middlemen and distributors. By and large, they've done a very good job, and while they take their cut of the price for their work (as it should be), the dealers in this hobby are perhaps more than any other hobby, honest people who love the books, know their stuff, and don't mind sharing their knowledge with fellow collectors and fans. It's a good group of people.

Another good place to buy collectible books is at science fiction conventions and collectible paperback shows. There are many SF, Fantasy, and Horror conventions (cons) all across the country, and some offer better material than others. Obviously a con that stresses print media (books) will offer a better opportunity to find good books than a pure Star Trek or video-related con. Nevertheless, I wouldn't dismiss any con; you'll be surprised what you can find, and often at a nonbook con you can pick up good books at very reasonable prices simply because the dealers don't specialize in these items or they may just want to move them out fast. In either case you're the winner and could pick up some very good books on the cheap.

Specialist paperback collector shows, such as my own annual New York Collectible Paperback Expo, while not as numerous, are serious book-related cons for collectors and are essential to the dedicated book collector. These shows (listed elsewhere in this volume) feature dealers who are book dealers *only*. There are often a hundred thousand or more collectible books on sale and display at these shows. And while dealers there sell books in all genres, the main thing is that all the dealers there are competing with each other for your money. So from a pragmatic point of view such shows are the best place for any serious book collector to be. They're essential. A lot of great bargains can also be found—especially if you know what to look for. The tips found in this book will be a big help to you in that regard. The contacts and information gained at these shows can also be invaluable. And lastly, these shows are just a lot of fun. There's nothing like them for the true fan, book lover, or collector.

Careful and intelligent buying at collectible paperback shows can actually stretch your budget. Buying unwisely at auctions—where the reverse market force holds true, where each buyer is in competition with each other for that one book they are bidding on—can bust a budget. This can sometimes cause large (and often inflated) prices. Auctions are a great device for the collector but they should be participated in carefully so they do not bust your budget. Or your pocketbook.

A BRIEF HISTORY OF COLLECTING PAPERBACK SF/F/H/

In the beginning of what was termed "the Paperback Revolution," when Pocket Books launched upon an unsuspecting public their first 10 titles in 1939, science fiction, fantasy, and horror were not the popular, lucrative, and separate publishing categories they are today. This was true even though two fantasy titles were included in that first crop of the original 10 Pocket Books.

Science fiction, while published for decades in the pulp magazines, was looked down on as "that Buck Rogers stuff" and had been left to the pulp magazines by book publishers of that era. There were some small press and specialty limited editions, highly prized by collectors today, but back then SF published in book form was a rare occurrence.

Mainstream hardcover and later paperback publishers stayed away from the SF genre. They didn't see it as a separate marketing and

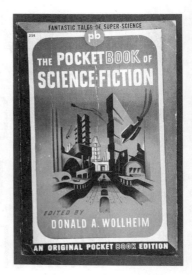

The Pocket Book of Science Fiction *edited by Donald A. Wollheim (Pocket Book #214, 1943),* early SF anthology and first paperback to use the term *"science fiction."*

publishing category then. It wasn't regarded as important (i.e., lucrative) enough for serious treatment.

It wasn't until 1943, with the publication of *The Pocket Book of Science Fiction* (Pocket #214), edited by Donald A. Wollheim, that the term "science fiction" was first used on a paperback book. It would be another decade before science fiction became a serious marketing category for paperback publishers—and not until the 1970s when it would become so for mainline hardcover publishers and begin to boom.

Regarding fantasy and horror, these genres did have a long and rich literary history. For instance, horror, more specifically supernatural horror and ghost stories, had been around for a long time and had a rich heritage in the publishing arena. There were many acknowledged classics in this genre, but not until the advent of *Dracula,* by Bram Stoker, did horror really become a legitimate form of serious literature on its own. In the past horror wasn't the scary, often excessive blood-and-slash genre work that much of it is today, post-Stephen King. The roots of horror literature gave us the model to create a more modern and logical way to explain our world and its phenomena, often in a nonreligious context.

Only in one magazine, *Weird Tales*, did genre horror develop with classic stories by then contemporary writers like H.P. Lovecraft, Robert Bloch, Clark Ashton Smith, Seabury Quinn, August Derleth, and many others. *WT* also included a good dose of fantasy and horror by Robert E. Howard, with his now classic Kull and Conan stories. However, as a separate publishing category for books, the horror publishing field, per se, did not exist until about 1980. The field exploded in the late 1970s with the Stephen King paperback boom. Before then, most of the better work, classics as well as new books, was often marketed as science fiction or fantasy. Meanwhile, horror authors from Bloch to Matheson were usually thought of early in their careers as science fiction authors and not what they really were—fantasy or horror authors.

Fantasy fiction has the longest tradition, a serious literary and historical line that goes all the way back to *The Odyssey* by a Greek named Homer, probably the original heroic fantasy quest novel (one of the prime sub-genres of fantasy). The King Arthur legend, Don Quixote by Cervantes, and *The Canterbury Tales* by Chaucer are other traditional themes from the Middle Ages that would be returned to time and again in fantasy fiction.

However, fantasy did not come into its own as a separate publishing category until the late 1960s or early 1970s. This new and relatively recent awareness of fantasy began with the popularity of J.R.R. Tolkien's *The Lord of The Rings* trilogy (and *The Hobbit*), and Robert E. Howard's Conan novels (12 paperbacks published by Lancer Books, later by Ace Books). These collected all the original Conan stories by Howard and added some new pastiches by other writers. They were all immensely popular. From that point on, fantasy in paperback has grown as a genre and as a publishing category. Today, genre fantasy fiction has exploded onto the paperback racks to such an extent that (aside from

INSTANT EXPERT

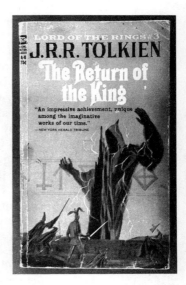

The Return of the Kings by J.R.R. Tolkien (Ace Books #A-6, 1960s), third in the Lord of the Rings series, unauthorized and later pulled by Ace.

romance fiction) it now dominates the fiction field.

The pioneer days of paperback publishing for these three imaginative fiction categories, science fiction, fantasy, and horror, tell three separate and distinct stories up until 1952, with the advent of Ace Books and Ballantine Books. Ace and Ballantine were the first true genre paperback publishers and the first to use science fiction as a separate marketing category. These were the first paperback specialists in science fiction publishing.

Before Ace and Ballantine came on the scene there were the wild pioneer days of the fly-by-the-seat-of-your-pants paperback publishers. This was a fascinating time when some of the most interesting science fiction, fantasy, and horror books (and some of the most expensive and key to collect) were published. We'll take a look at some of them now.

THE PIONEER DAYS OF THE HORROR PAPERBACK

While what constitutes horror (especially by today's standards) can be a bit eclectic, I've tried to stick as close to basic horror as I can in this short

The Werewolf of Paris *by Guy Endore (Avon Books #354, 1950), classic werewolf novel with great cover.*

examination of the pioneer paperback days of the genre.

I believe the first horror book published as a mass-market paperback was *Tales and Poems of Mystery and Imagination* by Edgar Allen Poe (Pocket Book #39, 1940), which features a mixed bag of classic Poe treats. Also that year, Nathaniel Hawthorne's weird Gothic/horror novel *The House of the Seven Gables* (Pocket Books #52, 1940) appeared. A year later, appearing for the first time in paperback, was what is perhaps the best werewolf novel ever published, *The Werewolf of Paris* by Guy Endore (Pocket Books #97, 1941). This was later reprinted by Avon Books (#354, 1951) with a stunningly classic werewolf cover, and in Canada by tiny Studio Pocket Books (#105, 1952) with a gorgeous good-girl-in-danger photo cover. In any edition, this is a collector's classic and an excellent novel. In Fine condition the Pocket edition could set you back anywhere from $30 to $100; the Avon edition about $30 to $45; and the Studio Pocket edition about $50.

During World War II, an outfit was set up to publish and distribute books to our military men overseas. These Armed Service Editions (ASE's) were often sideways paperbacks (usually rack-size but bound at the short end) and the list contained a good number of classic horror that appeared in paperback for the first time ever. These were published from about 1943 to 1947. The Armed Service Editions' earliest horror paperback was also a collection by Poe, this time titled *Selected Stories from Edgar Allen Poe* (ASE #J-297, also reprinted as ASE #767 later on). Next came their first novel in the genre, *Dracula* by Bram Stoker (ASE #L-25, also later reprinted as ASE #851). This is a much sought after book and a centerpiece for any horror collection. This was followed by another ASE that is a somewhat obscure and scarce paperback collection of stories, *Sleep No More* (ASE #R-33), by August Derleth, well-known Lovecraft fan and publisher. There was also a semi-horror novel in the series by Richard Sale, *Not Too Narrow . . . Not Too Deep* (ASE #S-7).

Moving on to the classic stuff: *The Dunwich Horror and Other Weird Tales* by H.P. Lovecraft (ASE #730) is a true gem and a first edition of this particular collection. It is a highly prized item and in Fine condition could cost about $100.

Another horror classic that appeared in this distinguished series was *The Strange Case of Dr. Jekyll and Mr. Hyde* by Robert Louis Stevenson (ASE #855), which was also a first paperback printing of this classic novel. Another ASE that could surely fit into this category is a very scarce and desirable item, *The Great God Pan and Other Weird Tales* by Arthur Machen (ASE #940). This is a first edition in paperback and an incredible collection by a neglected master of horror. Scarce, and in Fine condition it could set you back at least $50.

Tiny Bart House is a long-forgotten and obscure paperback publisher of the 1940s. They're not remembered for much these days except for recognizing the power and terror in the work of a fellow named H.P. Lovecraft. In 1944 Bart House published a paperback edition of *The Weird Shadow Over Innsmouth* (Bart #4, 1944), the cover showing

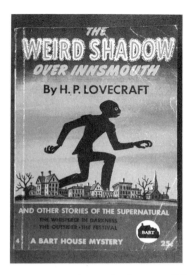

The Weird Shadow
Over Innsmouth
*by H.P. Lovecraft
(Bart House, 1944),
early horror novel.*

a strange giant shadow walking through one of Lovecraft's dilapidated New England towns. This may be the first-ever appearance of Lovecraft in paperback, probably predating the ASE edition mentioned previously. In Fine condition this goodie can run anywhere from $40 to $75.

A year later Bart House struck again to the delight of Lovecraft collectors everywhere with *The Dunwich Horror* (Bart House #12, 1945). This one features a simply terrible cover (not scary terrible, but just plain bad) showing a scared man and a dog at an open door. This book will cost about the same price as the previously mentioned book, but it isn't seen as often. These Bart House editions are both highly collectible: not common, but they are available.

Another even more obscure paperback series was the Quick Reader Books. These were small paperbacks, about 3" × 5" in size and running 128 pages. Nevertheless, there were two great horror classics in this series: the first was *The Best of Edgar Allen Poe* (Quick Reader #140, 1945); while the other is *The Strange Case of Dr. Jekyll and Mr. Hyde* (Quick Reader #142, 1945). These have nice pulp-inspired or comic-book type cover art and can go for about $25 to $45 in Fine shape. They are available but they are highly prized by many collectors because of their stunning cover art.

In 1947 three important horror paperbacks were published by various publishers. The first was Bram Stoker's classic novel *Dracula* (Pocket Books #452, a reprint of the earlier ASE #L-25). The next was a great short story anthology edited by Herbert Williams, *Terror at Night* (Avon Books #110, 1947). It has a magnificent man-girl-monster cover by George Meyers. This anthology contains work by such horror masters as H.P. Lovecraft, M.R. James, Lord Dunsany, Ambrose Bierce, W.W. Jacobs, Bram Stoker, and others. It's a scarce item in really nice shape. It seems this early horror anthology was widely read, so you don't often see many unread-Fine copies around. If you do find one in that shape, it will probably have a $50+ price tag on it. The third of the great horror paperbacks of 1947 was H.P. Lovecraft's *The Lurking Fear and Other Stories* (Avon #136, first edition 1947), with a magnificent A.R. Tilburne cover showing a ghoul in a graveyard that's become a kind of horror classic. Avon later reprinted this collection as *Cry Horror!* (Avon #T-284, 1958) with a nice Richard Powers

In the Grip of Terror *(Perma Books #P117, 1950s)*, early horror anthology with lurid girl-in-peril cover art.

skull cover. Avon #136 is getting hard to find in really nice shape, and it's very much desired by collectors—all paperback collectors as well as specialist Lovecraft collectors. The Avon #T-284 is still around, and at a substantially lower price, but Avon #136 I feel has to be *the* Lovecraft paperback for the Lovecraft collector and fan. Avon #136 in Very Good would cost about $40, in close to Fine condition perhaps $75; Avon T-284 goes for about $15 to $20 in the same condition.

We'll end this look at pioneer horror paperbacks with one of my all-time favorite anthologies: *In the Grip of Terror*, edited by Geoff Conklin (Perma Books #117, 1951), which features an absolutely incredible cover showing a really creepy guy gripping a terrified woman from behind. A ghoulish and delightfully pulpish cover for the outside of the book, while inside the book is classic work by Lovecraft, Poe, Wells, Collins, Crane, Bradbury, Sayers, Bierce, Saki, and others. A good basic horror collection and an underrated and underpriced paperback that is still available. Often you can pick this beauty up for as little as $10 in VG, and perhaps $15 to $20 in Fine condition.

This now brings us to 1952, which ends the pioneer phase of paperback horror published during the early vintage years.

THE PIONEER DAYS OF THE FANTASY PAPERBACK

The first true mass-market fantasy paperbacks were published by Pocket Books in 1939. That year, Pocket came out with four outstanding reprint selections: *Lost Horizon* by James Hilton (Pocket #1, their first book!), mythical Shangri-la lived in print and on the silver screen with Ronald Colman; *Topper* by Thorne Smith (Pocket #4), ghosts come back to haunt and humor an old gent; *Green Mansions* by W.H. Hudson (Pocket #16), a female Tarzan in the South American jungle; *Pinocchio* by Carlo Collodi (Pocket #18), a wooden puppet who wants to be a real boy; and *A Christmas Carol* by Charles Dickens (Pocket #29), presenting the ghosts of Christmas Past, Present and Future. All classic fantasy, then and now. These are not generally thought of as genre fantasy. They're certainly classic literature *now*, but they also *were* the bestsellers of their day. Bestseller fantasy novels! These were fantasy novels before a true fantasy genre had yet been born.

For collectors: *Lost Horizon* (Pocket #1) is a rare book, and would set you back about $100 to $200 in VG condition (we are talking first printing *only* on any of these books). *Topper* (Pocket #4) would set you back about $100 to $125 in VG shape; the other Pockets mentioned above would probably set you back about $50 to $75 in VG to Fine condition.

After this incredible start, Pocket Books slacked off a bit on fantasy for a few years. When they came back to it, it was with the popular Thorne Smith titles, sequels to the popular *Topper: Topper Takes a Trip* (Pocket #209, 1943); *The Passionate Witch* (Pocket #401, 1946); and *The Night Life of the Gods* (Pocket #428, 1947). Later on there was also a Pocket Books edition of *A Connecticut Yankee in King Arthur's Court* by Mark Twain (Pocket #497, 1948). These are valued at about $15 to $20 in VG to Fine condition and are often available in a variety of conditions and prices.

A year after Pocket Books began publishing its fantasy classic reprints in 1939, early fantasy paperbacks were also being published by a small and obscure publisher known as L.A. Bantam (no relation to Bantam Books). They published a series of small-format paperbacks especially for sale in vending machines. The idea didn't catch on but there are a lot of very collectible and scarce (many actually rare) books in this series. In fact, it could be said that almost every book in the entire L.A. Bantam run is scarce or rare. They all command high prices and are very collectible. They can fetch prices from $100 to $1,000+ in VG to Fine condition, depending on the title, especially if the book has an illustrated cover. Of all their books, the L.A.

Bantams that concern us here are *Grimm's Fairy Tales* (#16, 1940), a collection of short stories; *The Shadow and the Voice of Murder* by Maxwell Grant (#21 and #21p) in both text and pictorial cover versions (one of the pictorial covered versions recently sold at auction for over $800); and *Tarzan and the Forbidden City* by Edgar Rice Burroughs (#23 and #23p, 1940), an abridged version also in both text and pictorial cover versions (the pictorial version being more scarce and valuable).

After the early Pocket Books titles and the L.A. Bantams, we take a jump over to the Armed Service Editions (ASE's), where a slew of interesting fantasy paperbacks were published for the military from about 1943 to 1947.

The Armed Service Edition list of fantasy paperbacks was impressive and began with Lord Dunsany's *Guerrilla* (ASE #Q-14, later reprinted as ASE #954). Thorne Smith shows up here, too, with the first paperback edition of his *Night Life of the Gods* (ASE #S-28). H. Rider Haggard appears with two classic lost-race fantasies, *King Solomon's Mines* (ASE #795), and a bit later on with *She* (ASE #881). Thorne Smith checks in once more with *Rain in the Doorway* (ASE #922) and again with *The Passionate Witch* (ASE #953), which would later be reprinted by Pocket Books. A later ASE that is on the borderline between science fiction and fantasy was *Mr. Adam* by Pat Frank (ASE #1217). There were also two Tarzan paperbacks in this series by Edgar Rice Burroughs, both of which are highly prized: *Tarzan of the Apes* (ASE #M-16 Tarzan novel #1) and *The Return of Tarzan* (ASE #O-22, the sequel to the classic novel). These Burroughs titles are very scarce and very much sought after by collectors. They can run you about $75 to $300 depending on condition and are rare in the higher grades.

We'll now shift our focus to Avon Books. Avon began publishing fantasy in 1942 with their digest-sized Avon Murder of the Month series (later Murder Mystery Monthly, or MMM) and began with #1, *Seven Footprints to Satan* by A. Merritt. Merritt was a one-man fantasy factory for Avon, and they published all his work in various editions, formats, and reprintings all through the 1940s and 1950s. A. Merritt's work *was* fantasy for most readers in those early paperback days. All Merritt editions are collectible, but the first paperback editions (and digest editions) are the earliest and most collectible of all. They're also the most desirable because they have better cover art.

Merritt's many titles include *Seven Footprints to Satan*, which would be reprinted in 1943 in regular mass-market paperback size as Avon #26, and later again with a new and stunning cover in 1950 as Avon #235.

Most of the Merritt titles were also reprinted as part of the regular Avon series, and still later in the Avon T series. They were very popular and had print runs of 100,000 copies minimum. We will not look at the books in the Avon T series here as it was a later series and outside the scope of this section, but there are nice later reprint editions in this series and they're also quite collectible. Don't pass these up if the price is right. You should be able to get most of them for as little as $4 to $10 in nice condition.

The next Merritt Avon was *Burn Witch Burn* (Avon MMM #5, 1942), which was later reprinted in 1944 as Avon #43, and still later in 1951 as Avon #392.

Creep Shadow Creep (Avon MMM #11, 1943) has a very effective cover, a monstrous creeping shadow of impending doom. The book was also reprinted in 1947 as Avon #117.

The Moon Pool came next (Avon MMM #18, 1943). It was reprinted in 1951 as Avon #370.

Dwellers in the Mirage (Avon MMM #24, 1944) was the next book, and it featured much improved cover art by Paul Stahr. The book was reprinted in 1952 as Avon #413, and it was the last Merritt title to appear in the regular Avon series.

The Face in the Abyss (Avon MMM #29, 1945) contained another stunning Paul Stahr cover. As far as I can determine this book was never reprinted as part of the regular Avon series, but did appear in an Avon T edition years later.

The Ship of Ishtar (Avon MMM #34, 1945) was one of Merritt's most popular novels, and it also had a great Paul Stahr cover. It was later reprinted in 1951 as Avon #324.

The Metal Monster (Avon MMM #41, 1946) is a paperback original (PBO) with a beautiful cover painting. This was later reprinted as Avon #315 in their regular series and as Avon T-172 still later.

The last of the nine Avon Merritt titles was *The Fox Woman and Other Stories* (Avon #214, 1949), a first edition collection that was not reprinted until the 1980s.

In Very Good (VG) to Fine (F) condition most of the Merritt Avon Murder Mystery Monthly digests are available but can run you from $10 to $30. The Merritt paperbacks in the regular Avon series cost a bit more, from about $20 to $50. The Merritt paperbacks in the Avon T series go for about $4 to $10. These are all nice books and quite collectible for a variety of reasons. These books are big with fantasy and science fiction collectors because of their stunning cover art, and are popular with most paperback collectors in general.

Avon Books also published fantasy paperbacks by other authors besides A. Merritt (seems unlikely, but it is true). Avon published an edition of *The Stray Lamb* by Thorne Smith (Avon #69, 1945). Later they came out with *The Daughter of Fu Manchu* by Sax Rohmer (Avon #189, 1949), featuring a gorgeous Ann Cantor cover of Oriental menace right out of the old pulps.

Avon continued publishing fantasy fiction with its Avon Fantasy Readers, an anthology series of 18 digests that ran from 1947 to 1952. These marvelous digests showcased some of the best of classic fantasy stories, most of them reprinted from the pulps. The cover art was incredible: gorgeous women, terrible monsters, and stalwart heroes in bright-colored cover paintings made these books popular with readers back then and just as popular

INSTANT EXPERT

Avon Fantasy Reader #17, typical 1950s sword and sorcery cover.

Avon Fantasy Reader #13 with a more sexy science fictional cover.

with collectors today. The editor was Donald Wollheim. Wollheim made this an excellent series that was far ahead of its time. Available years ago for as little as $3 or $4 apiece, today most Avon Fantasy Readers are getting prices in the $20 and $30 range for strict VG to Fine condition copies.

The next entry is from a rather unlikely location. Staid and conservative Penguin Books (the British arm of this publisher would not even allow illustrated covers on their books) published *Out of This*

World (Penguin Books #537) in 1944. This is a classic anthology of fantasy stories edited by Julius Fast. Though the title would seem to indicate science fiction (and there are a few borderline SF tales here), the main thrust of this book is decidedly toward fantasy and the fantastic—with stories about deals with the devil, ghosts, a dog who works miracles, etc.—a very early and unusual anthology from a source you'd not usually think of. Not all that common, but not pricey either. It could probably be had for $5 to $15 in nice shape.

From the middle 1940s to 1952 there were many good fantasy paperbacks being published from a variety of publishing houses. One of these is: *The She-Wolf and Other Stories* by H.H. Munro (Bantam #143, 1945, in dust jacket), an excellent fantasy/horror collection, and with a nice condition dust jacket scarce and highly collectible. A VG to Fine copy might run from $75 to $300.

In 1950 three interesting paperbacks appeared from three different publishers. They were all excellent, but were very different types of fantasy books. The first was *Shot in the Dark*, a short story anthology edited by Judith Merrill (Bantam #751, PBO 1950). This featured a stunning cover by H.E.

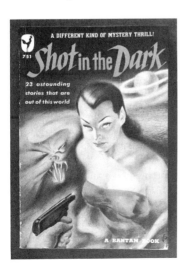

Shot in the Dark *(Bantam Books #751, 1950s), classic SF anthology edited by Judith Merrill.*

INSTANT EXPERT

The Dying Earth *by Jack Vance (Hillman Book #41, 1950), the classic book and Vance's first book!*

Bischoff of a gorgeous feral woman. Also in 1950, this time from Dell Books, was *Cleopatra's Nights* (Dell Books #414, 1950), edited by Allan Bernard. This one features a gorgeous and sexy Cleopatra cover by Ray Johnson.

The really important paperback of 1950 (in fantasy and in SF) was the publication of *The Dying Earth* by Jack Vance (Hillman Books #41, first edition 1950). Often termed a novel, this is actually a collection of interconnected and previously published short stories published as a novel. The important thing is that this was Vance's *first* book! It was an instant collector's item even at the time of publication, and today it is even more highly collectible. It is a prize in any fantasy or SF collection. The book turns up on auction catalogs sometimes, but true Fine condition copies are scarce. In moderate Very Good condition the book could easily set you back $100.

In 1951 Avon Books returned to the fantasy book publishing scene with *The Saturday Evening Post Fantasy Stories* (Avon #389, 1951), featuring a nice and colorful cover by William Randall. The *Post* and other "slicks" of the era occasionally published science fiction and fantasy (usually only the best stories of their day or by the better or most popular writers), and this anthology contains some fine gems and a couple of obscure ones. For some reason this book doesn't show up that often in really nice shape. It's usually a $10 to $15 book in VG.

This brings us up to 1952 and ends the pioneer phase of vintage fantasy paperback publishing.

THE PIONEER DAYS OF THE SCIENCE FICTION PAPERBACK

Most of the early pioneering science fiction paperback books, anthologies, and novels were experiments, some only published because of the hard work of a persistent fan and editor like Donald Wollheim. Wollheim's impact on paperback science fiction (and the paperback publishing scene in general) has been sadly neglected.

Other science fiction books, such as the work of H.G. Wells and Jules Verne, while already classics, were not really thought of as genre SF at all. After all, they *were* classics! However, in actuality they were the science fiction bestsellers of their day.

The first thing to remember about early science fiction is that there wasn't much of it published in books (paperback or hardcover) in the early days. Science fiction until 1952 was not a separate marketing genre for paperback publishers. Science fiction wasn't considered a viable book category as were the mystery or western genres. That was to soon change. Science fiction was still big in the pulp magazines (where most book publishers thought it should remain), but with the SF boom in the early and middle 1950s, it would soon transform itself into an SF boom in the paperbacks as well. As the pulp magazines emitted their last gasp, Ace and Ballantine Books were born to take their place. However, before the advent of Ace and Ballantine Books in 1952, there was an earlier pioneer time for the science fiction paperback that we'll take a look at now.

The first science fiction paperback (the first one

to use the actual term "science fiction") was *The Pocket Book of Science Fiction* (Pocket Books #214, 1943), an anthology edited by that ground-breaker of the genre, Donald A. Wollheim. This is a key book in the genre and historically significant. It is often available, usually at a reasonable price of about $20 to $30.

The first science fiction *novel* in paperback was probably *Rebirth* by Thomas Calvert McClary (Bart House #6, 1944). This is also a first edition novel in paperback; it reprints a novel originally published in *Astounding*. The cover blurbs states: "When machinery ran wild—when order became chaos—bedlam uncontrolled. The greatest escape story of the decade." This one is harder to find and can set you back $20 to $45.

The Armed Service Editions (ASE's) of World War II, given free to our troops fighting around the world, were cheap books made to be read in a foxhole, in the barracks, or on ship and then be passed around or thrown away. While there were many books in this series that are marginally SF (some of which may actually fit better into the fantasy or horror genres), there are still many fine classic SF titles in this series. Published from about 1943 to 1947, early ASE's were bound sideways, at the short end, but later editions were in the more familiar mass-market rack-size format.

One of the earliest ASE science fiction books was *Donovan's Brain* by Curt Siodmak (ASE #O-8). Others in the series were: *The Time Machine* by H.G. Wells (ASE #T-2); *The Island of Dr. Moreau* by H.G. Wells (ASE #698); *The War of the Worlds* by H.G. Wells (ASE #745 and later reprinted as ASE #1091); *When Worlds Collide* by Philip Wylie and Edwin Balmer (ASE #801, later also reprinted as Dell #627 in 1952 with a nice Robert Stanley cover); and finally *The Food of the Gods* by H.G. Wells (ASE #958). Of course the best and most collectible ASE and one that is quite scarce is *The Adventures of Superman* by George Lowther (ASE #656), a first and only paperback appearance. This

The Girl with the Hungry Eyes *(Avon Books #184, 1949), early SF anthology edited by Don Wollheim.*

one is rare in Fine condition and could go for as much as $300 to $600 in that grade. It was recently reprinted, but this time in an expensive hardcover.

By the late 1940s Avon Books took over the mantle of publishing paperback science fiction, marginally so to be sure, with their A. Merritt reprints and then in all its "sense of wonder" and glory in 1949 *The Girl with the Hungry Eyes* (Avon #184), another excellent anthology edited by Donald Wollheim. This one's a real beauty, science fiction packaged with a sexy good-girl fantasy cover (GGA good-girl art). It can cost from $25 to $50 depending on condition.

In 1949 Avon also published its first two science fiction novels in their regular series: *Out of the Silent Planet* by C.S. Lewis (Avon #195) and *Gladiator* by Philip Wylie (Avon #216). These can run you about $20 to $35 in solid VG condition.

In 1950 and 1951 Avon continued with science fiction by publishing a bunch of gorgeous and very collectible paperbacks. One of the best was *Into Plutonian Depths* by Stanton A. Coblentz (Avon #281); and C.S. Lewis' *Perelandra* (sequel to his *Out of the Silent Planet*). Both of these books feature incredibly wonderful and weird cover art right out of a pulp magazine dream (or nightmare) and can go for from $25 to $60 in nice shape.

The classically beautiful cover art gracing *An Earthman on Venus* by Ralph M. Farley (Avon Book #285) is a major reason for the popularity and desirability of this book with collectors. It's a pretty big money book today, and in Fine condition it can sell for $100 to $200.

There were only two books published in what was called the Avon Fantasy Novels series (but they really were SF). They're both great, classic SF and feature exquisite cover art. *The Green Girl* by Jack Williamson (Avon Fantasy Novel #2) is the tougher of the two and a real gem. It can cost about $75 in VG to Fine. *The Princess of the Atom* by Ray Cummings (Avon Fantasy Novel #1) is more common. While this book has a nice good-girl SF cover, the art does not approach the cover art on *The Green Girl*. This book would cost about $25 to $40 in VG to Fine. These are two very nice classic SF novels.

As if all this wasn't enough for Avon to handle in 1951, they also came out with *The Avon Science Fiction Reader*. This was a digest anthology series that ran only three books. A year later #2 and #3 came out. This is an interesting series, often mistaken for a magazine, and hence undervalued by collectors. It's an uncommon Avon digest series. These books go for about $15 to $20 in VG to Fine condition.

Of course other paperback publishers also got into the science fiction publishing act, getting their feet wet as soon as it looked as if SF would become a viable market. In 1947 Dell published a nice edition of *The First Men in the Moon* by H.G. Wells (Dell #201), which features some good lunar cover art by Earl Sherman.

Later on, in 1951, Dell Books would publish the first paperback by one of the greatest science fiction writers of all time. This was *Universe* by Robert A. Heinlein, which appeared as #36 in the Dell Ten-Cent Series. This was a first edition with a great two-headed mutant cover by Robert Stanley that's a classic of SF art. This one's a keeper; in nice shape

The Green Man *by Harold M. Sherman (Century Books, 1948 digest), early SF novel in paperback.*

it can go for anywhere from $50 to $100. It's a pretty book and an absolute must for any SF collector or Heinlein fan.

The Dell Ten-Cent Books, or "Dell Dimers," were thin, about 60 to 70 pages, stapled rack-size books featuring novelettes or short novels. There are 36 titles in the series and they contained all genres. They are very popular with collectors. The Heinlein book was the only SF book in the series, but it is an important and desirable book.

Not to be outdone by Avon and Dell, tiny Century Books joined the science fiction publishing scene and published a few very highly collectible titles in this pioneer era. Very significant for this short study is Century Book #104, *The Green Man* by Harold M. Sherman, a first edition in paperback from 1946. This is an early SF novel published in paperback (in digest size) at a time when less than a dozen such novels had been published in paperback. While that book was published in digest format, not traditional mass-market size, it is an attractive and scarce book. It can set you back about $75 to $150 in VG to Fine condition.

Century Books continued their noble SF experiment with two novels by Rog Phillips: the earliest

INSTANT EXPERT

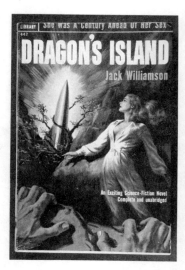

Dragon's Island
by Jack Williamson
(Popular Library
#477, 1950s),
classic Earle Bergey
SF cover art.

was *Time Trap* (Century #116, a paperback original from 1947). This time the book was in mass-market rack-size, and it was also the true, first-ever science fiction paperback original (PBO) novel. It sports an incredible and sexy good-girl-with-three-eyes cover. She's holding some kind of ray gun that looks more like a flashlight than anything else. A fun cover and a real sexy beauty. A true Fine condition copy could run you about $75 or more. A VG copy perhaps $40. This is one you'll want to own in the best condition possible. It's simply a gorgeous book!

In 1950 Century Books published a second book by Rog Phillips, *Worlds Within* (Century #124, PBO 1950). This time the book had a very sexy girl in a space suit cover. Cover art on both Phillips books were by Malcolm Smith. *Worlds Within* in VG to Fine condition could run about $30 or $40.

By 1952 there was a big change on the way for science fiction paperback publishing. Ace Books and Ballantine Books were just beginning their massive output, specializing for the first time ever in science fiction. More publishers also got on the SF bandwagon, and more anthologies were on their way, such as Perma Books' *Beyond the End of Time*, edited by Fred Pohl (Perma Book #P145), with a

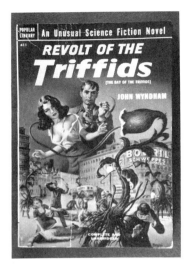

Revolt of the Triffids *by John Wyndham (Popular Library #411, 1950s), another classic Bergey SF cover for* The Day of the Triffids *(original title).*

nice "end of the world" cover. Other novels, such as *When Worlds Collide* by Philip Wylie and Edwin Balmer (Dell Books #627) also came out in 1952. This one was a reprint of the earlier ASE edition but this time with an excellent Robert Stanley cover. There were also more reprints from Avon Books, more A. Merritt titles, both in the regular Avon series and in the later Avon T series. There were also a couple of gorgeous Popular Library titles to take note of, both with classic Earle Bergey cover art: *Dragon's Island* by Jack Williamson (POP #447, 1952) with an incredible girl and spaceship cover that's become a kind of GGA classic, and *Revolt of the Triffids* by John Wyndham (Pop #411, 1952), this time with a man and woman attacked by giant maneating plants! Great pulp SF. They are two exquisite editions of these very good books and are still quite available. In nice shape they usually run about $20 to $40 each.

Pre-1952 vintage paperbacks—science fiction, fantasy, and horror—were the innovations, the very first beginnings of the modern genre paperback that we all enjoy today. They're fun to collect, and from such humble and inauspicious beginnings . . . a great industry arose.

INSTANT EXPERT

SF/F/H in the Later Vintage Era: 1952–1970

Books from the later vintage era and on into the mid and late 1960s are highly collectible today. Some of the best SF/F/H paperbacks ever published appeared during this era.

This was the heyday of Ballantine Books, when they began publishing science fiction paperback originals (and the incredibly scarce and highly priced Ballantine hardcovers). It was also the era of the now classic Ace Double Novels (the well-remembered "D" series, and later on their "F," "M," and "G" series). Berkley Books added to the scene with some nice editions of the SF novels and collections of J.G. Ballard and many other authors, most with covers by Richard Powers. Berkley published such Ballard classics as *The Wind from Nowhere*, and many of these were first U.S. editions, or first editions for that particular title. All very collectible titles today in the SF area.

This later vintage era also contained work published by Lion Books with their own small but important SF/F/H output (as well as some great crime titles by Robert Bloch and Richard Matheson

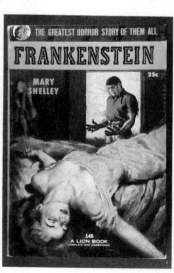

Frankenstein *by Mary Shelley (Lion Books #146, 1950s), classic SF novel gets the pin-up girl treatment on the cover.*

Collecting Science Fiction and Fantasy

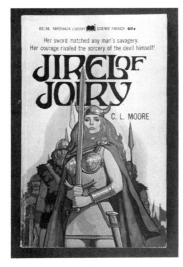

Jirel of Joiry
*by C.L. Moore
(Paperback Library
#63-166, 1960s),
early sword and
sorcery tales of female
warrior by female
author.*

Four from Planet 5
*by Murray Leinstar,
Gold Medal #937,
classic SF cover by
Paul Lehr.*

that are also highly collectible). There were also early science fiction and fantasy novels by Fritz Leiber and Damon Knight.

There were wonderful SF novels and collections from Gold Medal Books, most of them PBO's such as Murray Leinster's *The War with the Gizmos* (GM #s751), and *Four from Planet 5* (GM #s937). Then

INSTANT EXPERT

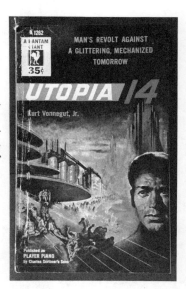

Utopia 14 *by Kurt Vonnegut, Jr. (Bantam Books #A1262, 1950s), early version of his SF novel* Player Piano.

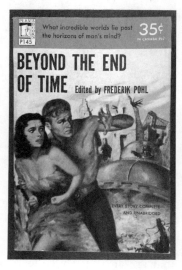

Beyond the End of Time *(Perma Books #P145, 1950s), early SF anthology edited by Frederik Pohl.*

there were Richard Matheson's two great SF-horror novels: *I Am Legend* (GM #417, 1954) with a great Stanley Meltzoff cover, and *The Shrinking Man* (GM #s577, 1956; reprinted in 1962 with reduced cover art by Mitchell Hooks as #d1203). All great stuff and highly collectible.

COLLECTING SCIENCE FICTION AND FANTASY

Perma Books and Pocket Books (which would purchase Perma during this period) did a number of fine anthologies that are highly collectible also. My own favorites are *In the Grip of Terror* (Perma Books #117, a great horror anthology), edited by Geoff Conklin, and *Beyond the End of Time* (Perma #P145, a great SF anthology) edited by Fred Pohl. *Science Fiction Terror Tales* edited by Geoff Conklin was another great SF anthology, this time published by Pocket Books.

Ray Bradbury's *The Martian Chronicles* also first appeared in book form during this period from Bantam Books, as well as many of the great science fiction and fantasy novels (and crime novels as well) by the great Fredric Brown, all very much sought after.

Dell Books, which had pretty much neglected SF in the early days, came out with some interesting items during this period. These included John W. Campbell's *Who Goes There and Other Stories*, featuring "The Thing from Another World," which became a major motion picture and was recently remade by John Carpenter as *The Thing*. And the Jack Finney classic, *The Body Snatchers*

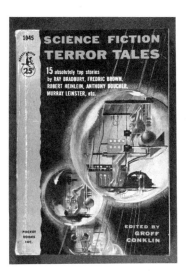

Science Fiction Terror Tales *(Pocket Books #1045, 1950s), early SF anthology edited by Geoff Conklin, with Stanley Meltzoff cover art.*

INSTANT EXPERT

Two "after the bomb" novels: Hero's Walk *by Robert Crane (Ballantine #71, 1950s) and* Alas, Babylon *by Pat Frank (Bantam Books, 1950s).*

The Body Snatchers *by Jack Finney (Dell First Edition #42, 1950s), the first book appearance.*

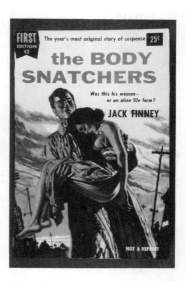

(Dell First Edition #42, 1955, with a great John McDermott cover) was made into two rave film versions as *Invasion of the Body Snatchers*.

There were many more classics of the period: some of the high points were *Alas, Babylon* by Pat

48

Frank and *A Canticle for Lebowitz* by Walter M. Miller, which had big cult followings. These were two excellent end-of-the world novels in which civilization has to rebuild itself. A bit later, when a Cold War hysteria brought nuclear fear, there were novels such as *Fail Safe*, *On the Beach*, and political thrillers like *Seven Days in May* and *Dr. Strangelove* that were popular and made into hit films.

Later on in the 60s, Anthony Burgess's *A Clockwork Orange* and Robert Thom's *Wild In the Streets* (Pyramid Book #X1798, PBO 1968) were books that had a big impact and were also made into popular counterculture films of the era.

The 60s was not only the decade of classic SF/F/H films (with the accompanying tie-in paperbacks of course), but also of classic SF/F/H TV (with its own paperback tie-ins). Shows like "Star Trek," "The Wild Wild West," "Batman," "The Green Hornet," "The Addams Family," "The Munsters," "Lost in Space," "The Twilight Zone," "Voyage to the Bottom of the Sea," "Land of the Giants," and "The Time Tunnel" all had their own paperback tie-ins. Fantastic spy shows like "Get Smart," "The Man from U.N.C.L.E.," and "Mis-

A Clockwork Orange
by Anthony Burgess (Ballantine Books #U5032, 1960s), predates Kubrick film.

INSTANT EXPERT

Wild in the Streets
*by Robert Thom
(Pyramid Books
#1798 PBO, 1960s),
classic film tie-in.*

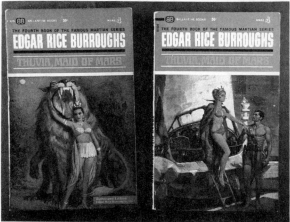

Variant covers for Thuvia, Maid of Mars *by Edgar Rice Burroughs (Ballantine Books, 1960s).*

sion Impossible," which often had SF or horror elements also had their own paperback tie-ins. It was a Golden Age for the paperback tie-in and for fans of these classic films and TV shows.

Important books that first appeared during the 1960s or attained cult following in that era are leg-

COLLECTING SCIENCE FICTION AND FANTASY

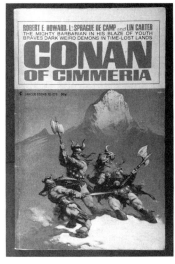

Conan of Cimmeria *by Robert E. Howard (Lancer Books, 1960s), early Lancer reprint, cover by Frank Frazetta.*

end and quite numerous. These are just a few: *Stranger in a Strange Land* by Robert A. Heinlein (remember "Grok!"?), *Psycho* by Robert Bloch, *Dune* by Frank Herbert, the Conan books of Robert E. Howard, the revival of Edgar Rice Burroughs' Tarzan and Mars novels in paperback, and the exquisite horror stories of H.P. Lovecraft and Clark Ashton Smith. Philip K. Dick was at the height of his powers, J.R.R. Tolkien was getting hot with a book called *The Hobbit* and a trilogy of novels called *The Lord Of The Rings*, while Richard Matheson, Charles Beaumont, and Rod Serling were writing their hearts out for an anthology TV show called "The Twilight Zone." Meanwhile, on another station "The Outer Limits" brought us a monster a week, but also the Zanti misfits and "Demon with a Glass Hand" (by Harlan Ellison). It was a good time.

Many of the paperbacks of the later vintage era are heavily collected today and a lot of interest has surfaced in all books of the 1960s. These later vintage paperbacks are a very hot area right now and one that has still not peaked in collector interest and investment.

INSTANT EXPERT

The Late 70s Science Fiction Boom

It all happened quite unexpectedly. Science Fiction was going along in the 1970s as a rather slow but somewhat stable genre, old-timers leaving the field, one way or another, and young turks yet to make their mark. SF book publishing was on a flat line, some thought edging ever so slightly on a downward curve, others seeing a slight upward curve. And there were a lot of reprints. Then something came along in 1977 called *Star Wars*. The mega-hit film shook SF to its roots and shook Hollywood to its pocketbook (meaning where Hollywood keeps its money and some say its heart as well). *Star Wars* shook book publishers also.

Star Wars was such a big hit and (more importantly for SF) made so much money that suddenly SF became *big* business. More SF films were made, more SF novels were published in hardcover and paperback. Science fiction publishing programs were expanded significantly, and where they did not exist, they were quickly created. Every publisher began their own SF imprint. SF authors were now paid big advances and SF was big stuff. It was a boom time for SF. It had seen this boom and bust cycle before but this was the biggest and the best boom there had ever been.

From about 1977 to 1981 SF was the *in* thing in reading, and therefore for publishers. So many books were being published, many trying to capitalize in one way or the other on *Star Wars* (or a generic space opera formula, naturally without a word of thanks to E.E. "Doc" Smith who invented the genre), but many other good works also appeared (as well as a lot of junk). The Cyberpunk movement began at this time and became a major force in the field in the 80s and 90s. Many new and exciting writers came along to replace the old SF pros who were either too old or had passed away—though in some cases the boom (and the big advances it spurred) lured other old pros out of retirement and back to writing, resulting in the appearance of many big new books. It was an exciting time in SF publishing, and an exciting time to be an SF reader. An example of this was that after so many years (decades actually) fans were treated to new Foundation and Robot novels by Isaac Asimov, new books by Robert A. Heinlein, and more fine material from greats like Alfred Bester, Frank Herbert, John Brunner, L. Sprague de Camp, Harlan Ellison, Poul Anderson, Greg Benford, and many other big names.

THE 80S HORROR BOOM

Except for Bram Stoker and his one novel, *Dracula*, (and I'll leave out H.P. Lovecraft for the moment), no other author has had the impact on the horror genre as has Stephen King.

King's work, while appearing in paperback in the later 1970s, really hit its stride with readers in his paperback editions around 1980. Throughout that decade King was king and horror was King (and horror was king as a genre as well).

Of course there were other authors who also

Two collectible 1970s pulp horror series: The Frankenstein Horror series (Popular Library) and The Dracula Horror series (Pinnacle Books).

INSTANT EXPERT

Pet Sematary
*by Stephen King
(Signet Books), one of
King's many popular
novels in paperback.*

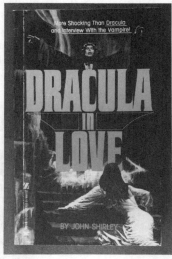

Dracula in Love
*by John Shirley
(Zebra Books, 1980s,
PBO), horror novel by
punk/cyberpunk
author.*

came along then, or who had been writing quality material in the genre for many years quietly and without much recognition, but that was also soon to change. Many of these authors also came into prominence as the genre grew and horror became *it* during the 80s. Writers such as Peter Straub and Robert McCammon, and from science fiction and

Two early Dean Koontz science fiction novels mixing fantasy and horror elements: Anti-Man *(Paperback Library) and* Warlock *(Lancer Books).*

fantasy (where his early works appeared in the 60s and 70s) there was Dean Koontz. Ramsey Campbell (one of his best books is *The Doll Who Ate Its Mother*), T.E.D. Klein, and Charles Grant contributed, as well as long-time horror masters such as Robert "Psycho" Bloch and Richard "Hellhouse" Matheson.

Nevertheless, Stephen King's work formed the foundation of the modern horror field, mostly among uninitiated mainstream readers who, looking for a thrill, turned to horror in the 80s in ever-increasing numbers. Cheap thrills, relatively, in a three or four dollar paperback. In some ways it might be said of the entire horror field during the 80s (and there is some truth to this) that it existed solely to offer readers additional thrills and spine-tingling chills to read while they waited for the next Stephen King (or Dean Koontz) book to be written and published. That's quite a mouthful, but there is truth to it, King's influence on the genre was incredible.

Naturally, such a boom produced a bandwagon effect and that meant there was a lot of schlock published in the 80s in the horror genre (especially in paperback by the smaller houses). However, there are also a lot of hidden gems here as well: first edition novels, first novels by now collectible authors, and many paperback originals (PBO's). Many of these command high prices today in the collector market and have no place else to go in value but up. Collectible horror paperbacks from the 80s are an untapped vein of gold for the knowledgeable collector because they were published so recently (relatively recently, that is), and it's still not widely known even by most book collectors what the good collectible books are in this area. Published in small print runs (some as low as 10,000 copies by the smaller houses), with often spotty distribution, there are many items from this era that are scarce and difficult to obtain today.

The horror paperbacks of the 80s offer an interesting challenge to the modern genre horror collector and to speculators and investors in collectible books. Many of these books have very good future value potential.

THE 90s FANTASY BOOM

Today in the 90s distinctions between genres have blurred quite a bit. Hard SF, while still being published, has been relegated to a relatively small niche in the SF cosmos. The horror boom has now faded because that market was glutted in the 80s. However, today, fantasy of all types is very popular and being churned out by paperback publishers at a (dare I say it?) fantastic rate!

These books include all manner of shared-world anthologies, cute anthropomorphized feline and other animal adventures, media and computer game tie-ins, alternate-world and alternate-history series, time-travel stories, and other material in anthologies, collections, and novels. It also includes classic novels with sequels written by other writers, and collaborative novels, sometimes even books where one author finishes the work of another who may be too old or has passed away.

In fact, we find ourselves today in a fantasy publishing boom (though some, especially more traditional or hard SF fans, see it as a glut on the market). In many cases there is a lot of inferior work produced today, very derivative work, and some just plain bad writing. There are derivative Marion Zimmer Bradley Darkover novels, derivative Conan novels by everyone *except* Robert E. Howard (the original creator), or J.R.R. Tolkienesque high fantasy quest novels written by a host of imitators who have no feel for the words and less for the flavor of language that was so important to Tolkien.

There's also an endless array of just plain bad books about lovely unicorns, evil gnomes, or fairy princesses. It can get to be a bit much, and yet mixed in with all this dreck are some really good books. Some are good from a collector's point of view, others from a reader's point of view. The problem is not that there isn't anything good out there, the problem is finding the good stuff.

My main complaint, however, with the current glut on paperback racks of derivative fantasy books (and I've heard this mentioned time and again by many fans and readers) is that these books take valuable rack space from other more serious, harder, or well-written science fiction books. Even classic reprints, which seem to come out with far less frequency than they used to, are good books with a proven track record and following. There seems to be a problem in fantasy land.

High fantasy, combined with much of the media-related tie-in paperbacks (such as *Star Wars*, *Star Trek*, computer and TSR Dungeons & Dragons type novels, various reprints, and all the theme and shared-world anthologies) leaves little room for actual new science fiction novels and PBO's.

Nevertheless, this is a cycle we are in that I think will change in the future. The Cyberpunk movement has already taken up some of the slack but I believe that a harder science fiction (a more hard-boiled futuristic SF with political overtones) will become a large part of this genre in the future. It will kick!

For now, however, fantasy is king in the 90s and with so many books being published in this genre, it is difficult to separate the wheat from the chaff. Since individual tastes can differ considerably, rather than just talk about what I "like" or what I consider is "good," or what may be popular because of a media tie-in or high sales, this book will look at books that collectors prize and the ones they are looking for and willing to pay money for. Many of these books are listed in the section on collectible SF/F/H paperbacks at auction elsewhere in this book or in the collectible books section earlier in the text.

THE STAR TREK AND STAR WARS PAPERBACK BOOM

Star Trek:

At one time (and it may be hard to believe), after the original "Star Trek" TV show went off the air in the 60s, you could not find any books to read about Star Trek. Oh, there were the James Blish Bantam Books paperback editions that adapted actual episodes from the original TV series (and one original novel by Blish, *Spock Must Die*), but that was all. It was just too little. Meanwhile, syndication of the TV show caused increased demand for new Trek material. There was a hunger out there that had to be fed. Well, that all soon changed. It also changed paperback publishing forever.

Bantam Books began first, building a small Star Trek paperback publishing empire in the 1970s by publishing original novels by recognized SF writers based on the original TV show. Many of these books are out of print today, though Bantam does reprint them from time to time, sometimes with new cover art. It is the first printings that are the originals and are the ones worth money. There are

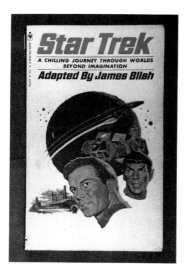

Star Trek *(Bantam Books, 1967), the first Star Trek paperback, contains adaptions of the original TV episodes by James Blish.*

many good books in this series for Trek fans to read for sheer enjoyment. They are also collectible.

Today, Pocket Books has taken over the Star Trek paperback publishing pastiche factory by publishing a few hundred books, original novels not only based on the original 60s TV show, but also on each of the three later incarnations of Star Trek: "Star Trek: The Next Generation" (ST:TNG), "Star Trek: Deep Space Nine" (ST:DSN), and "Star Trek: Voyager" (ST:V). There are also many non-series books, special sets, retellings of Trek history, novels dealing with the young Kirk or Spock (as well as each of the minor characters and newer ones in each series). In fact, almost every manifestation of the Star Trek phenomenon appears somewhere in one of these books.

Pocket Books, which at one time had a rather large and active science fiction publishing program (they published the excellent Timescape SF imprint) closed that down almost entirely and subsumed their SF publishing program into a Trek publishing program. It's been that way for almost a decade. They've published a lot of good (and some pretty mediocre) Trek books, but little else in the way of SF unless it is by the big names.

Star Trek is a phenomenon that just keeps on rolling along and shows no signs of slowing down in interest among fans—now worldwide. In fact, there is every sign that Trekdom is actually growing larger!

Paperback originals of key or popular books (Trek novels dealing with popular subjects like how Kirk and Spock met, etc.) or books written by top SF authors (many top SF authors are now writing original Trek novels, a kind of in-thing today that can be very lucrative) are the key books to have and save in nice shape. An increasing number of the newer key books are being published first as hardcovers, publishers wanting to get a bigger payday, but there are still plenty of the previous PBO editions out there, and many new PBO's still coming out every month are worthy of notice. Many of these paperback originals (and we are only talking about the first printings here) are already selling for $15 to $50 in some cases. The earlier Bantam PBO's can also sell for that much, and more in some cases. Again, only first printings are collectible.

The trend here seems to be ever onward and upward. Onward with more books and upward in price and value. With over 200 PBO's already published on various incarnations of Trek, these books are an incredible paperback publishing story and offer collectors much opportunity. Many of the earlier books in the Pocket and Bantam series are out of print and command good prices in the collector market already. There is a continual demand, and while reprints appear frequently, I get the feeling that the publishers, at least in this area, are having trouble keeping up with that demand.

Star Wars:

A similar situation, though on a much lower level and with far fewer tie-in books published, occurs with the Star Wars paperbacks. Part of that is because the Star Wars tie-ins began later, they're really an 80s phenomenon. Of course that first Bal-

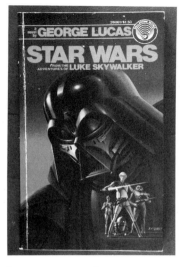

Star Wars *by George Lucas (Ballantine Books #26061, PBO, 1976), predates film,* cover art by Ralph McQuarrie.

lantine PBO of Star Wars by George Lucas from 1976 that predated the release of the first film is a money book in nice shape. It's the very first Star Wars book! In fact, since it came out before the film, it's the very first *anything* about Star Wars! It has historical significance as well as collector interest.

Later books, various tie-ins with the three films, and many original novels that expand upon, or continue, the story have also appeared and are quite collectible. Especially important are PBO's that are not tie-ins with the films but are original novels expanding the story or continuing the adventures of Luke Skywalker, Lando Calrissian, or other heroes of the films. Many of these books continue the story in a time frame after (or in some cases before) the films took place. All of these books are very collectible and show great potential for the future. Many of the earlier books are also out of print and avidly sought after by fans and collectors.

Star Trek and Star Wars are two incredible phenomena, and the paperback originals that these two series have spawned are books that fans will be collecting for decades to come. This fandom, rather than ending because there has been no new *Star*

INSTANT EXPERT

Wars film for some time, or because the original "Star Trek" TV show has been run into the ground in syndication, is not ending but actually growing. It has yet to attain its full potential. And while lately some of the bigger or more important books in these two sub-genres of SF publishing have been appearing first in hardcover, there is an abundance of excellent PBO's out there that (in first printings) are true future collectibles. So stock up now!

SF/F/H MOVIE AND TV TIE-IN PAPERBACKS

These paperback tie-ins are incredibly popular with readers and collectors. It's a genre (and some may say mini-art form) all its own. The tie-in book has grown up and grown out of mass-market paperback publishing in an explosive manner. It was made possible because paperback books can be published far more quickly and targeted to their core audience more easily than hardcover books. These tie-in paperbacks have become very collectible in recent years.

Tie-in paperbacks will become even more col-

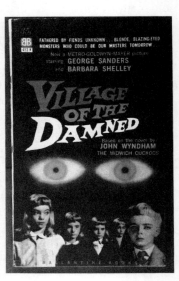

Village of the Damned *by John Wyndham (Ballantine Books #453K, movie tie-in edition), based on his novel* The Midwich Cuckoos.

Burn Witch Burn *by Fritz Leiber (Berkley Books, 1960s), classic movie tie-in of his novel* Conjure Wife.

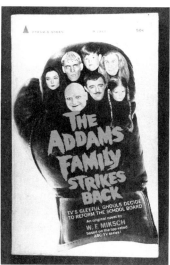

The Addams Family Strikes Back *by M.F. Miksch (Pyramid Books #R1257, PBO 1960s), tie-in with classic TV series.*

lectible in the future. And why not? With covers featuring the biggest stars of Hollywood and the small screen, about the hottest and most popular hit films and TV shows, these are images instantly recognizable nationwide (and, increasingly through cable and satellite, now worldwide). These books cannot miss with fans and collectors. Since almost

INSTANT EXPERT

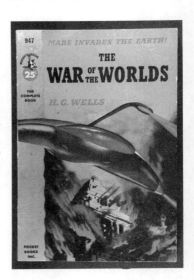

The War of the Worlds *by H.G. Wells (Pocket Books #947, 1950s), cover ties in with the George Pal film.*

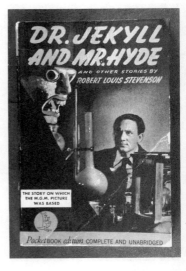

Dr. Jekyll and Mr. Hyde *by Robert Louis Stevenson (Pocket Books, 1940s), classic movie tie-in with Spencer Tracy on the cover.*

all these books were published originally in paperback, paperback collectors have gotten the jump on everyone else and have been after them for years. They know a good thing when they see one. Now the general public and media fans are beginning to go after them too.

SF/F/H TV and movie tie-in paperbacks from

COLLECTING SCIENCE FICTION AND FANTASY

Psycho *by Robert Bloch (Crest Books, 1960), movie tie-in edition with the classic Janet Leigh photo cover.*

Land of the Giants *by Murray Leinster (Pyramid Books #X1846, PBO, 1960s), TV tie-in novel.*

films like *Gorgo, Reptilicus,* or *Star Wars,* to TV shows like the original "Star Trek" or the recent hit "The X-Files" are instant collectibles. A TV tie-in for the recent NBC TV show "Dark Skies" may be a very good book *if* one is published. I feel that one could appear soon, probably by the time you are reading this.

INSTANT EXPERT

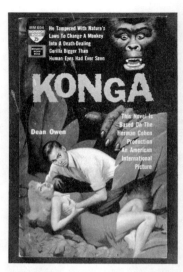

Konga
*by Dean Owen
(Monarch Books
#MM604, PBO,
1960s), classic movie
tie-in novel.*

The X Files:
Whirlwind
*by Charles Grant
(Harperprism, 1995),
top horror author does
tie-in novel to hit TV
series.*

Tie-ins with both vintage and current films and TV shows are the books that may soon blast the collectible paperback hobby into a boom that it has never seen before. Tie-ins are very popular with all people (not just collectors or SF/F/H fans). Even people who do not read at all, or do not collect, like to own the tie-in book for a favorite TV show or film. They will usually cherish that book, just as they do the memories of that film or TV show, and usually pay a good price to own it.

Classic 60s TV, and 50s and 60s SF/F/H films are instant hits, campy and nostalgic, and the paperback tie-ins with them are collected by many people and are in great demand. The field shows only signs of growth and expansion for the future.

Think and Talk Like an Expert

THE IMPORTANCE OF CONDITION

The prime aspect of any collectible (and this proves equally true for collectible SF/F/H paperbacks as for anything else) is the actual physical condition of the item. Books in unread condition, or as close to new and unread condition as possible, are the ones collectors want and the ones they will pay big money for. Collectors and even dealers will often pay a premium price for the older vintage era (1939–1965) books in that better condition. Of course, these older books, especially in the higher grades, are often scarce.

The Warren and Hancer paperback price guides (listed elsewhere in the Reference section of this book) give a detailed examination of condition in various grades, ranging from Mint (M) to Good (G). Some of these grades are misleading and unnecessary concerning paperbacks. Mint, especially, is actually a comic book collector term, not a book term. The term Mint (M) has almost no application to vintage paperbacks. There are, essentially, no Mint condition vintage books. Fine is the standard highest grade in the field. So I've kept it simple by using the three basic grades that almost all advanced collectors and specialist dealers use: Fine (F), Very Good (VG), and Good (G). Obviously, there can also be gradations within a grade, such as F- or ABT F (About Fine), or VG+, VG-, or even G+. Some of these gradations can also be a bit dicey at times. What's the difference between a VG- and a G+? Probably not much, except a book described as VG- may sound better than a book that's a mere G+. So you see there can be some flexibility in how some of these grades are determined.

Nevertheless, collectors and dealers with experience in the field are often very strict in their grading and often bend over backwards to ensure that books are described properly and accurately graded. It's a matter of professional pride and good business sense to keep their customers happy and never disappoint them on book purchases.

More than any other consideration, the condition of the book has become the primary determinant of its value—even more than its importance as a "key" book or "hot" item that collectors are avidly seeking.

Let's take a look at the three grades of condition:

FINE (F)
This should be the highest grade for a collectible paperback. This is, essentially, an "as-new" book. It will have white pages, no spine roll, no cover creases, no cover fading or tears, strong and tight binding, absolutely no loose pages or loose cover, and no cover marking or writing of any kind. There will not even be the normal or general wear that is seen on most books of the vintage era. A Fine condition book was probably never read, or might have been read just once very carefully and then put away. There will be no defects on a book in this condition.

This condition is uncommon in paperbacks of the vintage era (1939–1965). Collectors of books of this era must often accept a lower grade book such as an F- (with one or two very minor defects), a VG+, or a VG copy because the supply of actual F copies is so limited.

Paperbacks from the 1970s onward, because of their relative recent publication, often higher print runs, and better distribution, are required by most collectors to be in a minimum of Fine or F- condition. Most of the books from this later and more recent era are available in these higher grades.

Generally, paperbacks of the 1960s fall into an in-between area. Too few reference books or price guides have adequately addressed the books from this decade so some information and pricing can be sketchy, but this decade already contains many hotly sought after books. The 1970s and 1980s offer prime areas for future paperback collectibles. There are many hidden gems lying out there, especially in the lower-end publishers such as Zebra, Manor, and others. Just remember, the better the condition, the better the book will hold its value or even enhance its value.

VERY GOOD (VG)

This grade, with its gradations of VG+ and VG- (also ABT VG, about VG, or Solid VG), takes in a lot of territory. The main thing to remember here is that this is the minimum condition acceptable most collectors and dealers will accept for a collectible book. The only exception to this may be on some of the high-priced "key" editions. These are often used as "fillers" until a better grade of book comes along to replace it in the collection. Dealers usually stay away from anything in less than Solid VG condition.

Very Good condition books often have a variety of minor defects, or even one of two more major defects. These can include almost everything not allowed as a defect in a FINE condition book (listed above). Paperbacks in VG will always be complete books, there will be no missing cover (also including back cover), no loose cover or pages, nor any missing interior pages. The book will be complete and readable.

A VG- book may show signs of regluing, excessive wear in spots, such as the spine, a small cover hole or tear(s), cover writing, stronger spine roll, or larger reading crease. Defects on a VG- book will be more pronounced than on a VG book.

There are a variety of defects in VG condition books. These should be relatively minor flaws but there may be up to three or four of them. Taken as a whole, the defects should in no way equal more than any one major defect. Other defects can include: overall general wear, light scuffing to book spine or edges, or minor scuffing on the cover, a minor cover crease or two, or one large cover crease that will be the only defect (and a major one at that!), a sticker on the cover that can be carefully removed, a bookstore stamp inside, a previous owner's plate on the inside. There can be a slight spine roll, a remainder cut, a small tear (not a disaster if not on the front cover), a torn interior page, a small reading crease, very light warping or a back cover stain (a front cover stain would mar the cover art and bring the book down to a VG- or a G). One or two of these defects could easily bring the book down to a VG-, while more severe wear or damage will cause it to drop to a mere G copy. In many cases, since the cover art is often so important to the collectibility of any book, anything that mars or damages the cover or the cover art (even a minor defect) can often seriously affect the collectibility and value of that book.

GOOD (G)

First, while the term is called Good, that does not mean it is a "good book" for collectors. It's not. Books in this grade, while complete, are often far too heavily worn or damaged for any serious collector (or investor/collector) to include as a permanent part of his or her collection. Some collectors do keep some Good condition copies as fillers (especially on key books that are rare or highly expensive) or as reading copies, or just because a better grade copy of that book might be so scarce or too expensive. The collector may not want to, or may not be able to, pay for a better copy. It all depends. Collectors, like everyone else, have their budgets, and a successful collector will adhere to that budget carefully. For some collectors who do not care about condition (and there are plenty of these), Good copies are a very inexpensive way to obtain copies of books that may be otherwise unattainable. People on limited budgets or fixed incomes often collect Good copies; some completist collectors accept Good copies in their collections. Some old-time collectors who actually read all the books and love them as fans and readers, collect Good condition copies. They care more about what is *inside* the book than the way it *looks*. What a concept!

There is nothing wrong with any of this. However when, or if, it comes time to sell your books (perish the thought, no true collector can conceive of such a day!), it will be a lot easier and you'll be able to make a more lucrative deal if you're selling a VG or VG+ condition collection versus a Good collection. The harsh truth is that you may not even be able to sell a collection of Good condition books to a dealer. You might have to eventually give many of the books away, or worse and perish this thought, throw the books away. It's all too terrible to contemplate but if all your books are in this low grade (essentially fillers or reading copies), the only solace might be that you probably paid next to nothing for them in the first place. If that's so, at least you've read and enjoyed the books, and had the pleasure of owning them for a time. When it comes time to pass them on to another, you'll find you're still ahead of the game. My one caveat is just don't expect to make a killing when you put books in this low-end condition on the market.

There are many good reasons why people collect Good condition copies, and there is nothing wrong with collecting books in this grade. They're just not items that will appreciate in value. If you can live with that as a collector then Good copies can be a real bargain and a great source of reading and collecting pleasure.

How to Grade a Paperback

Now that you know the three basic conditions of paperbacks, we'll take a look at how to grade the books. Grading is a bit of an art and a bit of a science all rolled up into your basic guestimate. It's also a very important aspect of any book valuation, and it's necessary for any book seller or buyer to have books graded correctly and accurately. It often takes time to build this knowledge. It may take years of experience before a person can grade a book properly. Of course, there are some dealers in the business for many years who still do not seem to properly grade their books, even now. Of course, that is a prime consideration for anyone thinking of purchasing a book from them. These sellers are generally well known (or perhaps notorious, may be a better word) since the field is small and news (good or bad) travels fast. Conversely, there are dealers who consistently grade accurately, including some newer or younger dealers. They are often serious and careful businesspeople, or people who have come from the ranks of the collecting community themselves. They're collectors too. And readers.

There are a lot of things to look for in grading a paperback, and you should refer to the previous section on condition where I have listed some of the defects used in determining condition. But proper grading is less a mere listing of every defect than an incisive collector's interpretation of the sum of the book's parts. In other words, is the book a desirable piece and is it in collectible condition? Would you (the person grading the book) accept such a book for your own collection in that condition? Or would you use it as a filler?

Your opinion of the book, your grading of its condition, tells a lot about the book and also your own collecting habits and personality. Is this a book you can sell? Okay, fine, but is it a book you can proudly pass on to a fellow fan or collector for him or her to appreciate and cherish? You see the difference? Selling books, like anything else done well, can often approach art, and it can mean a lot more than it appears to be on the surface. Collectors and fans cherish these books and many regard themselves as keepers of a sacred object—a good book—which is an important and respected ideal, as it should be. It is especially true among book people. Bookselling is not just selling books, it's passing on books and knowledge to people you like and care about who share your interests. It's a kind of brotherhood and sisterhood and it can often bind people together just as tightly (and sometimes more so) than the pages of these books are bound together.

There is also a tendency for some collectors, many who love books too much, to overgrade and sometimes overcharge. These people are good and honest dealers but often are overzealous collectors, maintaining their collector mentality when they've become a dealer. Dealer mentality is far different than a collector's. In any case, these people don't stay in business long. They usually don't sell many books at the higher prices, and if they do, their overgrading will leave a lot of customers disappointed. These dealers also can get a lot of books returned for refund if they have been improperly graded. Some collectors can be real sticklers for condition and will not accept anything less than what is actually stated as the condition of the book.

The reverse situation also exists. There are collectors who are such fans, they are eager to share their love of SF/F/H with others. Sometimes these collector/dealers undergrade their books and sell them at very low, even ridiculously low, prices. Accurate grading is an important aspect of the book hobby and is crucial to bookselling. It's a learning experience and a learned experience, and the key is to develop a good eye in inspecting the book and a

INSTANT EXPERT

keen awareness of the flaws that most collectors can live with and those that most collectors cannot live with on a prospective book purchase.

Accurate adherence to the definitions of what constitute a Fine, Very Good, and Good book are essential as well.

As I said, it's a bit of an art and a bit of a science. It can also be a lot of fun when it is done correctly.

MARKET TRENDS

There are certain constants in the paperback collecting world, and we'll begin with those. Paperback originals (PBO's) are hot, and if you have PBO's in the higher grades by a classic collectible author that is something you want to aim for.

Let's take a look at a PBO published by Gold Medal Books in the 1950s, *I Am Legend* by Richard Matheson. This was Matheson's first book, a novel, and a classic horror and SF story. He's a very popular and collectible author, the book is scarce in condition, it's a popular, in-demand collectible, an SF-zombie novel, and a PBO. In Fine condition this would be a gem. What could be better?

I Am Legend *by Richard Matheson (Gold Medal #417, PBO), cover by Stanley Meltzoff.*

Each aspect of the previous statement describing that Gold Medal edition of *I Am Legend* is important for its collectibility and value. The fact that you have such a combination of excellent factors makes this book highly collectible. And valuable. Such a copy in Fine condition could run from $100 to $250. Such a book has the possibility of going even higher in value. Since Matheson is still alive and has even done signings at some collectible paperbacks shows, a signed copy could increase the value of the book by 10 percent to 20 percent. These signed copies will further appreciate upon the author's death. Collectors and investors are aware of this grim reality, and for me to ignore it in this book would mean that I wasn't doing my job. Even though they may be big fans of these authors and their work, and often personal friends as well, collectors, dealers, and investors understand that these authors will not live forever and that copies of their books that are signed (or have good inscriptions) do go up in value upon the author's death. Signed copies by authors who do not sign many books are always prized. Usually it's just simply supply versus the demand.

SF/F/H are perennially popular and collectible fields, so the market will always be volatile and active, and there will always be action and interest in the better paperback collectibles in this area. Prices on key books in Fine shape can only go higher and higher. And since paperbacks as a rule are very much undervalued presently (that may all change, probably at the turn of the century, a mere four years from now!), these books will be even more prized as collector's items someday. Then almost all paperbacks published "Last Century" may become hot collectibles. This will be at a time when we'll probably have only electronic books from the major publishers (such plans are in the works even now).

In the meantime, look for the best condition books, books by classic authors, and with artwork by collectible artists. Look for an author's first book and, especially, PBO's. Pick up better condition TV and movie tie-ins, especially from popular TV shows and films of the 60s and 70s. Certain authors with cult followings like Philip K. Dick have books that will only increase in value. Dick was primarily a writer of paperback originals for Ace Books and other outfits in the 50s and 60s. His PBO's are hot now and will only go up in value. Robert Silverberg is very underrated as a collectible author. Ironically his high volume of non-SF and soft-core adult material written in the 60s under a pseudonym has made him very collectible, and this will carry over into his SF work. (By the way his SF work is just excellent: read his *Up the Line* for a truly memorable time travel novel.)

There are many women worth watching, and their books are already hotly collected. Marion Zimmer Bradley, C.J. Cherryh, Rebecca Orr, Anne McCaffrey, Joanna Russ (her *The Female Man* is a classic and is much sought after), Emma Bull, and Ursula LeGuin, are just a few. Also Poul Anderson, Richard A. Lupoff, of course Michael Moorcock, and many other men and women too numerous to mention. Naturally Star Trek, Star Wars, Dr. Who, and pulp-related paperbacks (such as Doc Savage Gooks), all in first printings only, will always be good bets.

In fantasy and horror there are many excellent books that are very collectible now and will only go up in value in the future. First printings or PBO's by Robert E. Howard, H.P. Lovecraft, and J.R.R. Tolkien are avidly collected, as well as books about these authors and others. Ace Books #D-36, *Conan the Conqueror* by Robert E. Howard from 1953, is the first-ever Conan paperback. The three Ace pirated editions of J.R.R. Tolkien's Lord of the Rings trilogy, and the Beagle/Boxer (as well as Ballantine Adult Fantasy) editions of all of H.P. Lovecraft's work are also being collected avidly.

The Ballantine Adult Fantasy series (with the Unicorn head) and the Ballantine Horror series (with the devil head) comprise a group of classic books in these genres that are very collectible and in demand. Many of the authors in these series are the best that fantasy and horror have to offer and their work is superb classic material not readily available before or after these editions were published; included are works by Lord Dunsany, George MacDonald, Clark Ashton Smith, William Hope Hodgson, James Branch Cabell, and many others.

More recent horror and fantasy novels by Ramsey Campbell, Brain Lumley, Clive Barker, Orson Scott Card, Tom Dietz, Dan Simmons, Tom Disch, Thomas Ligotti, and others are very good collectibles. Many are also PBO's, and the authors are fine writers who do good work that I feel will stand the test of time. And that's always important for any collectible work. Of course books by Stephen King, Dean Koontz, Joe Lansdale, and Robert McCammon are always collectible as well.

The six thin paperbacks published in 1996 as *The Green Mile* by Stephen King, a serial novel in six parts, first printings only, were collectible upon publication, actually before publication. *The Two Dead Girls*, the first of the six, in first printing only, is already tough to find and in demand. This is a good prospect and a set of all six paperbacks in first printings is quite collectible as a paperback original novel. Eventually, all six parts of the books will be combined into one edition and that too, will be collectible.

There is so much that is collectible in paperback fantasy and horror. This includes much mixed-genre work, SF mixed with horror (*I Am Legend* by Richard Matheson), fantasy with sword and sorcery with detective (*Darkworld Detective* by Michael Reeves; or The Garrett books by Glen Cook), and even Sherlock Holmes and SF (*Sherlock Holmes Versus the War of the Worlds* by the Wellmans). Pulp and comic-related paperbacks in the SF/F/H area are also hot and show good signs of going up in value: Batman, Superman, Marvel Comics heroes, or pulp heroes such as Doc Savage, or The Spider

INSTANT EXPERT

A Memory of Murder *by Ray Bradbury (Dell Books, 1st ed. 1980s), classic pulp crime story collection with a great pulp-inspired cover.*

(with eight great recent paperback first editions published by Carroll & Graf), and much more. Favorite authors who cross most genres include William F. Nolan, Ron Goulart, Joe Lansdale, Harlan Ellison, and Richard Matheson (Matheson's even done westerns, as has Lansdale, both mixing SF/F/H elements effectively). It's a wide open area with a lot of good material for the collector and reader, and most all of it is collected and in demand by someone.

BASIC VOCABULARY AND GLOSSARY

Advanced Reading Copies (ARC's): They do not contain a review slip, but are usually a copy of the actual book sent out in advance of publication to reviewers. It can be either bound galleys, or the actual book, but often with a different cover, usually without any illustration.

Backcover (or B/C): The reverse of the book, the part of the book cover that is on the back of the book.

Bookstore Stamp: Usually located on the inside front cover or the title page, an ink stamp with the name and address of a secondhand bookstore that sold the book at one time. A not-too-serious defect, but one that should always be noted.

Colophon: The special logo of a publisher, usually located on the spine of the book, or the bottom of the title page.

Completist: A type of collector who collects everything in a certain field or genre.

Condition: The particular grade of a book.

Cropped Cover Art: Art that has been cut or had a border placed around it. Usually this occurs on reprints where the cover art from the first printing is used on another printing but with a portion of it cut out or covered.

Cover: Refers to the front cover only, and includes all art and text thereon.

Cover Illustration: The illustration (artwork) on the cover of the book. This does not include other items on the cover such as text and logo, etc.

Dupes (Duplicate): Abbreviated term for duplicate copies of books in your collection. These are usually available for sale or trade at reasonable prices or terms.

Edges: The three sides of the book where the pages meet. Edges often were stained yellow, orange, or red on many of the vintage books to thwart insect pests.

Edition: Refers to a specific printing and binding of a specific publisher's book. It can be a reprint, a paperback or hardcover, or a first edition or first paperback printing, even a first printing by a reprint publisher.

Fair: A grade that is lower than Good, a reading copy or filler only, unacceptable for collecting purposes.

Filler: A lesser grade copy used to fill in a hole in a collection until a better copy is found. Usually only a Good or Fair (less than G) copy.

Fine: The highest grade of a paperback, near mint condition.

First Edition: The first time a book has ever appeared in book form. This can be in paperback or hardcover, but may be preceded by a magazine appearance.

First Paperback Printing: The first time a particular book has appeared in paperback. It may have had previous hardcover or magazine appearances but never a previous paperback edition before this one.

Genre: A sub-category of literature, or fiction.

GGA: Standard abbreviation for Good-Girl Art.

Good-Girl Art (GGA, or pinup art): Actually a comic book term for the sexy girl cover art that often appears on many vintage paperbacks and is prized by collectors (most of whom are male).

Good Nick: British slang term for a book in Good condition, usually meant as being in collectible condition, such as VG to Fine condition.

Grading: The art of determining the overall condition of a book as F, VG, G (or various gradations thereof).

Hot: Can refer to a book or an author, when there is very high demand or collector interest.

Key: A book that is scarce, rare, or has great demand or significance. It may be on a lot of want lists also.

Logo: An emblematic device of a publisher, also a Colophon.

Mass-Market Paperback: Actually this term refers to the method of distribution where returns are accepted for credit against future books. The system was created in 1939 and is still in use today.

Owner's Plate: An adhesive or glued-in label, "Ex Libris," stating previous owner's name, etc. Not a serious defect, but one that should always be noted.

Paperback Original (abbreviated as PBO): Refers to the edition of an original paperback book that has never before seen publication in any form. This includes any previous paperback printing, hardcover or digest appearances, or even magazine appearances. A PBO is always a first edition. However, not all first editions in paperback are PBO's. Some have previous magazine publication, so they are not entirely originals.

PBO: Abbreviation for paperback original.

Pseudonym: Or pen-name, or nom-de-plume. A name that a writer assumes and is published under that is not his true name. This is done for various purposes.

Publisher's Proofs: Called variously proofs, publisher's uncorrected proofs, or galleys, they can be bound or unbound, are usually uncorrected at this time before the actual publication, and are sent out early to critics and reviewers. The book is still in the editing stage at this point.

Reading Crease: On the cover of the book where it has been opened and creased for easier reading purposes. Usually a somewhat serious defect.

Reprints: Where the book has been printed again. A reprint can be in hardcover or paperback, and a book can be reprinted by the original publisher in a new edition or second printing, and also by another publisher. Reprints are always worth less than the original.

Review Copy (w/slip): A copy of the actual book published usually sent out with a review slip (see below) to reviewers and critics, a month or two before the book appears.

Review Slip: The publisher's slip inserted into and sent out with the book for reviewers before publication. It contains pertinent information about the forthcoming book, and it is the slip itself that has the value for collectors, not the book.

Spine: The part of the paperback where the pages are bound (usually glued) together.

Spine Roll: Curve of the spine of a book due to careless reading, generally a minor defect that can be corrected by gently bending the book to reverse the damage. Extreme cases can severely damage the book and are hard to correct.

Sticker Pull: The place where a price sticker has been removed, usually also removing part of the cover underneath or the lamination. A serious cover defect.

Want List (or Wish List): A list of books, usually by author and title, or sometimes by publisher number, of books you want to get for your collection.

Warp: From water damage the book will get wavy, or warp. It can also have water damage spots or stains that can be serious if on the cover and affect the cover art.

Water Damage: Wet books can be warped or stained and this can be a significant defect, especially if on the cover.

Worm Hole: Small holes in the cover or throughout pages of the book where egg-laying insects got into the book and their larva ate through it leaving a small hole.

THE WANT LIST

The want list or wish list is a good way to keep track of all the books you are in need of for your collection, and it can be very helpful when looking through large caches or dealer stocks of books.

Want lists can be as brief as a one-page handwritten sheet with a few books on it to pages of computer printouts or notebooks with dozens of pages and listings. The good thing about a want list is that many dealers (and even some advanced collectors) will find books for you from a want list if you let them have a copy. So make one up and spread it around and you might be surprised what may turn up. Always list the minimum condition of the books you are looking for, and while you are under no obligation to buy books people find for you from your want list, you should bear in mind that it can take considerable work and effort to dig up books on your list, so your want lists should be made up and treated seriously. Dealers that will accept and work off a want list are listed later.

YOU HAVE TO BE ABLE TO WALK AWAY

That is, you have to be able to walk away from a deal at times. You have to remember that except in rare cases (and with genuinely rare books, generally where there are less than 10 or 20 known copies in existence), you'll always be able to find that book somewhere else and sometimes at a better price. You just have to wait and have some patience, particularly if you do a lot of looking and networking with fellow collectors. If so, most vintage and all recent SF/H/F paperbacks will be available. After all, most of these books were printed in the tens of thousands of copies, if not in the hundreds of thousands of copies. So the odds are with you that any book, no matter how tough or elusive, will eventually show up. The exceptions to this are few and far between—the first 10 Pocket Books in first printings only, and most L.A. Bantams which are genuinely scarce to rare. Almost all other mass-market vintage and recent paperbacks are not. So patience can be a virtue and save you some money as well.

As my British friend Phil Harbottle recounted to me not too long ago about "Sod's Law," it seems that no sooner do you find and purchase an expensive collectible book on your want list, than you'll find another copy a week or two later at some yard sale for a dollar or so. Or in some thrift shop in the three-for-one-dollar bin. Naturally, according to this law, the new duplicate copy will be in far better condition than the copy you spent money for. These kinds of silly things occasionally happen.

Best Condition is Always Best

That's a general truism. If you buy the best condition books, if you always try to get the book that's in the best shape, then that's the best thing for you and your collection. Here again, patience takes a hand, and rather than buy that much desired and dreamed about edition in VG, you may want to wait and hold out for a better VG+ or Fine copy. In many cases it actually pays to pass up an attractively priced VG copy for a superior copy in Fine condition, even when that Fine copy will cost you much more money. In some cases it is better to pay the extra money for a Fine copy because that is also the copy that will go up in value and price. Best condition is always best. And by the way, for some books, you'll just want the best condition copy that is available, or nothing less than a Fine copy will do.

Networking

Networking with other paperback collectors is extremely important for serious collectors. Establish a group of friends and contacts. You can build them through paperback shows and dealers you buy from, or from people who advertise in *Paperback Parade* and other sources. Get to know them, and what they collect, what they are looking for, what they have, and get to meet and know their friends in the hobby. Meet with a collector in your area and have him bring his or her friends to meet you. It can be a very rewarding experience. The more people you get to meet and know in the hobby, the better it will be, and it can be a lot of fun. Book people are an incredible and very diverse group of fascinating individuals. You'll enjoy meeting them.

How to Tell Reprints

With regard to most mass-market paperbacks, this is a pretty straightforward situation. You just have to look inside the book on the copyright page, on the back of the title page, where the copyright notice is. Here it will usually tell you the printing number and date of that printing. It may also state if it's a first printing and much other valuable information such as when the book was first published (if it had previous hardcover publication), and the date of copyright. Always check the book carefully; if the copyright date and the printing date do not match, then you could have a much less valuable (or even perhaps worthless) reprint on your hands.

Sometimes the copyright page will only list the latest (most recent) printing number and date. On newer books these are often listed with the printing number and date of the first printing only. Some books actually will make it easy and state "First paperback printing" and have a date listed, but you must check the printing number (or code) to determine if it's a first printing or a reprint. The print number usually lists a series of numbers that may read: "1 2 3 4 5 6 7 8 9" or "10 9 8 7 6 5 4 3 2 1". If it reads "2 3 4 5 6 7 8 9 10" but the book states "First Printing: Jan. 1988", then what you have is a *second* printing (without any printing date information for that reprint) of a book that was first printed in January 1988. If the book was originally a PBO, this later, second printing (reprint) will be worth substantially less. It may even be worthless as a collectible book and have value only as a filler or reading copy.

Some vintage publishers had long numbered runs of titles. Pocket Books, Popular Library, and Dell Books each published over a thousand books in their regular series. They made it easy, by starting their numbering with one and going up to number one thousand and beyond. Some of these books during the vintage years were reprinted, and they can be determined by the "1" placed in front of the book number. So if the original edition was number 438 in the series, the reprint would be listed as number 1438. This was a good way to code reprints, especially since most vintage reprints using this method of numbering were often identical to the earlier edition except for the new number. This system seems to have worked well up to the late 50s and into the early 60s. However, once the big publishers' series began to approach one thousand books, the possibility of confusion between new books just published with their higher numbers and reprints of older books became evident. Something had to be done. The system was discontinued altogether in the late 60s when publishers moved to the International Stock Book Number (ISBN) code.

Many publishers such as Ace Books and Avon also reprinted their books years later as part of their regular series with new numbers and sometimes new cover art, as if they were new books. Some publishers also changed titles on reprints to try and sell more books or make the reprint seem to be a new book when it was not. All of this adds interest to some of the reprints. With new cover art, new numbers, and sometimes new titles, we have new and different editions that are often interesting and sometimes even collectible. Some of these later reprints from publishers often feature stunning cover artwork by some very well respected and highly collected artists. Sometimes, the only reason these later reprints are collected at all is because of the new cover art, or the artist doing that cover art.

Gold Medal Books had an early numbering system that began with book number 101 (the series actually began with #99 and #100 but these books had no numbers) and continued far beyond the one thousand book number. These books had the printing number and date listed on the copyright page, and were usually pretty accurate early on regarding first printings if the book was a PBO. Later things got a bit confusing. Some Gold Medal reprints appear as later books in the general series with new numbers and sometimes new cover art as well. Still later, there was a complex code of dots used to determine if a book was a true first edition or PBO. As most Gold Medal Books were originals, it's important to collectors to determine if a book is a reprint or a PBO. Sometimes the only difference between the PBO and the reprint will be the price. The original may have no price (assumed to be 25 cents), or a 25-cent price on the cover, while the reprint may list 35 cents. Canadian editions also often have 35-cent cover prices and most say "Printed in Canada." These editions, while usually having smaller print runs, are often valued less than the U.S. editions they reprint.

Determining the various editions, printings, first editions, etc., of some of these books can be very difficult at times and the publisher's records in the books themselves are sometimes suspect. For example, various editions published by Ballantine Books in the 1970s, when they were an Intext company, are problematical because Ballantine's printing records on many books at that time are listed incorrectly.

Nevertheless, this is just the kind of bibliographic detective work that many book collectors and fans enjoy. The thrill of discovery can be a great feeling. Realizing that book you bought at a yard sale for a dollar is actually a first edition or a PBO from a hot author and is perhaps worth $100 or more can really make all the searching worthwhile. And of course, all that knowledge can pay off in cash.

Dealer's Lists: A Good Place to Buy

Overall, paperback dealers' lists are the best places to buy good books at good prices throughout the year. Naturally, there are better places to get good book deals. Paperback shows are the best places, but they're infrequent, usually only annual events. Estate sales and flea markets can net tremendous finds for paltry sums but usually only for someone with the time and energy to search and travel. However, even here good fortune is getting rarer and rarer. So overall, dealer lists offer the best, most diverse assortment of collectible books. If you peruse and buy from many specialist paperback dealers (rather than just one or two), you'll find their lists can also offer competitive prices. Many of the books on these lists will be easily within any budget the SF/F/H collector may have. A list of recommended specialist dealers appears later on in this book.

Foreign Editions

No book on collecting SF/F/H paperbacks would be complete without at least an acknowledgment of foreign editions. These break down into basically two kinds of books: books printed in English and those in older languages.

Books printed in English are books we can all read, (mainly British editions, but also Australian, Canadian, and other books from English language speaking countries). There are also some books from non-English speaking nations that are printed in English. The important thing that makes such books of greater interest is they can be read by collectors and fans in this country. A secondary bonus is that many of the best and most popular American authors have appeared in these editions.

The other category is foreign language books, which most Americans and collectors cannot read. These books, while interesting, and often with incredible cover art, are worth substantially less than English language editions.

While foreign editions form a tremendous body of work and could be the focus of an entire book all their own, they fall outside the scope of this book. Nevertheless, collectors should take note of the many fine editions of SF/F/H reprinted in the U.K.

from paperbackers like Digit, Corgi, WDL, Consul, Pan, Boardman, Scion, Curtis-Warren, and many others. Australian editions in the highly desired Scientific Thriller digest series, American Science Fiction series, Thrills Incorporated, and various Horowitz editions and series are always popular and highly collectible.

There are also many very nice and interesting foreign-language editions published in France, Italy, Germany, Sweden, and other European and South American nations.

Foreign editions not only offer the reader and collector a worldwide perspective on a favorite author or book, and a new or different perspective on cover art for those books, they offer an appreciation of the international flavor and beautiful diversity of all those books in whatever guise they appear.

All ABOUT PAPERBACKS

HOW AND WHY PAPERBACK COLLECTING BEGAN

People have been collecting ever since there has been "stuff" to collect. There is a real joy in collecting, and if you're a collector you know exactly what I'm talking about. If not, it's hard to describe, but collecting is like being a part of something big and important. It's about belonging and comradeship, and book collecting has a strong intellectual and scholarly base that often gives it a depth of meaning, importance, and satisfaction unlike that in any other collectible field.

Paperbacks—the modern mass-market books we all read and enjoy today—began with a special 2,000- copy trial edition of Pearl Buck's *The Good Earth* in 1938. Distributed only in the New York City area to reviewers and critics, the books were a huge success and the paperback publishing industry was born.

Once paperback publishing began, it was

not soon after that paperback collecting began. Basically people just read the books or held on to the ones they liked, forming their own library. For the first time in history a personal library was within the grasp of the common man because of the availability of cheap paperback editions.

Probably the first instantly collectible paperback was the Hillman edition of Jack Vance's *The Dying Earth* published in 1950. The book was a first edition (often incorrectly termed a PBO), and one of only a scarce handful of genuine science fiction and fantasy books published at that time. Vance was also a very popular SF writer even that early in his career—though some thought his name was another pseudonym for the very prolific Henry Kuttner.

The Dying Earth was in instant demand by SF fans, and since Hillman's distribution was spotty at best, the book became scarce in some areas almost as soon as it was published. Hence it became a prime collectible paperback even in 1950. Some book dealers back then were asking as much as one dollar for this, then new, 25-cent paperback. Today, the book can easily fetch prices of $100 or more!

Paperback collecting itself evolved out of science fiction and mystery fandom, but today has become its own field with its own history, magazines, reference books, scholars, and specialist conventions.

Collecting these books began in a variety of ways and for a variety of reasons. Early collectors often chose a favorite SF author or artist, topic or theme to collect. Others chose to collect *all* the SF paperbacks published (an easy task in the early days but quite impossible today). You can collect whatever you like, whatever interests you. More ambitious collectors choose a favorite publisher (Ballantine, Ace, Bantam, Pocket Books, etc.) and try to complete an entire run of all that publisher's books (science fiction and others). Completist collecting, even with a single major publisher (there are completists who collect *everything*!) can be a daunting and expensive task.

Some of the older or more advanced collectors have attempted (and a few have actually succeeded) in attaining complete runs of almost *all* publishers' paperbacks—usually from the 1939–1965 Vintage Era. These "completist" collectors set themselves a collecting task much akin to a life's work, and much of the knowledge and information we have today is due to their pioneering efforts. Today, such completist collecting, even for just one of the major publisher print runs, means a massive expenditure of time, effort, and cash. In the old days it wasn't so. As recently as a decade ago vintage paperbacks of all kinds were easily available at yard sales, book shows, estate sales, and even many bookstores for as little as ten cents to fifty cents apiece. In many cases vintage paperbacks actually sold below their original cover price (almost always 25 cents) or were just given away or thrown out in the garbage. Paperbacks, after all, like old comic books and baseball cards, were never intended to last in our disposable culture of the 1950s and 1960s.

The current paperback collecting field is a market and network formed by many specialized dealers, fans, collectors, and even authors and artists. There are special auctions of rare or scarce paperbacks. Magazines, like my own *Paperback Parade* (published since 1986), are specifically devoted to collectible paperbacks and the hobby, regional paperback collector shows, and many other events. And there are many beautiful old and new books from all over the U.S. (and increasingly from around the world) that are highly collectible and sought after. Prices can range from a bargain $5 for a decent shape 30- to 40-year-old vintage book to $500 or more for a key title in top shape. What you value all depends on what you like to read and what you like to collect. If enough people have the same interests, then you might have a trend, and the demand will create some hot books that might fetch some big money.

Science fiction, fantasy, and horror paperbacks include some of the hottest and most collected books today. The authors and artists in these fields are perennial favorites, many of them having developed followings over careers that have spanned decades. Older and harder-to-find editions of their work (especially from the 40s and 50s) in nice shape are always very desirable. Many of these books can go for big money, especially if they have a combination of winning factors: such as a Fine condition copy of an older or classic author's first book that also happens to be a paperback original, or one that was published in the 50s or 60s and may be uncommon in the better grades. The cover art will also be a prime consideration.

Paperback collecting has grown over the years into a very active and stable hobby that shows steady growth with more and more people entering the field every day. While it's not so large a hobby as other mammoth collecting areas (baseball cards and comic books, etc.), people who collect paperbacks are a small family of friends and book lovers. It's a fun hobby full of nice people you'll enjoy meeting and talking to about books. For a reader, there's nothing quite like it.

THE NON-COLLECTOR COLLECTOR

Like many other areas of collecting, there are many science fiction, fantasy, and horror fans and collectors with large collections of books who are not hooked into the hobby. They don't think of themselves as collectors, per se, but usually only as readers. They may or may not take part in book auctions, buy from dealer lists, or even subscribe to publications in the collecting field. They don't think of themselves as collectors, and in fact, for a variety of reasons, many of them are not actual collectors. What they are, however, is non-collector collectors. They often have large caches of SF/F/H books (on whatever their interest or speciality may be) and keep the books stored in a variety of conditions. Some keep the collection nicely stacked on shelves, each book individually bagged for maximum protection, others may just be hoarders who simply amass a large amount of paperbacks in an almost never-ending quest to fill their shelves or storage boxes. Almost all are readers.

The non-collector collector represents the non-active collector, and they are out there in the millions, like the unseen 90 percent of an iceberg. They are usually fans in the general reading public who may not be a part of any organized fandom but who also keep the science fiction, fantasy, and horror genres popular by continually buying the books they like by the authors they like to read. It is from these enormous ranks that new collectors, fans, and dealers are born and reborn.

50 Most Valuable SF/F/H Paperbacks at Auction

For the last few years the collectible paperback dealership Gorgon Books has published *Paperbacks at Auction*, a book listing the results of all paperback auctions. This includes the title, author, publisher, and number, and the actual dollar amount paid. Obviously the cooperation of all the auction houses involved is essential, and many of the better ones are listed elsewhere in this book. They are also highly recommended.

What follows is a list of the highest-priced books in the SF/F/H genres at auction, paperbacks that have sold for $100 or more. These figures come from the latest edition of *Paperbacks at Auction* from 1995. See the Reference section of this book for more information on how to order this fine book.

The prices below are actual prices paid in auctions in the period from 1991 to 1994 and give some indication of what these books are selling for. However, take these prices with a grain of salt as these are only auction prices, and values can rise or

INSTANT EXPERT

Cry Plague! *by Theodore S. Drachman (Ace Books #D-13, PBO, 1952), the first Ace SF novel— but not the first SF Ace Double.*

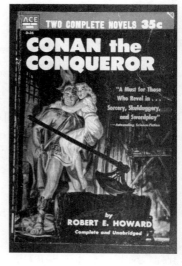

Conan the Conqueror *by Robert E. Howard (Ace Books #D-36, 1952), the first Conan paperback, cover by Norman Saunders.*

plummet depending on supply and demand. Also note that there are many thousands of paperbacks of all genres listed in *PAA* that sell in the $5 to $99 range.

The following list has many of the most collectible SF/F/H paperbacks and prices paid for them in VG to near Fine condition. They are listed

COLLECTING SCIENCE FICTION AND FANTASY

alphabetically by publisher just as they appear in *Paperbacks at Auction*.

Solar Lottery by Philip K. Dick (Ace #D103, PBO), $67.

Neuromancer by William Gibson (Ace #56950, PBO), $165.

Cry Plague! by Theodore S. Drachman, M.D. (Ace #D-13, 1953, first Ace SF novel), $121.

Conan the Conqueror by Robert E. Howard (Ace Books #D-36, first Conan paperback from 1953), $82.

Shooting Star by Robert Bloch (Ace #D-265, PBO 1958), $137.

The Naked Jungle by Harry Whittington (Ace #S-95, PBO 1955), based on the Charleton Heston film, $121.

20 Million Miles to Earth by Henry Slesar (Amazing Stories SF novel, no#, PBO 1957, SF movie tie-in), $165.

An Earth Man on Venus
by Ralph M. Farley (Avon Books #285, 1950s), classic and collectible SF.

INSTANT EXPERT

Time Trap
*by Rog Phillips
(Century Books, PBO,
1949), first
SF PBO novel,
features incredibly
sexy-girl cover.*

The Moon Pool
*by A. Merritt (Avon
Books #370, 1950),
incredible blonde and
giant frog cover.*

Adventures of Superman by George Lowther (Armed Services Edition #656), $275. First Superman paperback and very scarce.

Tarzan of the Apes by Edgar Rice Burroughs (Armed Service Edition #M-16), $117.

The Return of Tarzan by Edgar Rice Burroughs (Armed Service Edition #O-22), $550.

The Green Girl
*by Jack Williamson
(Avon Fantasy Novel
#2, 1950), great
two-book series with
incredible cover art.*

Murders in the Rue Morgue by Edgar Allen Poe (Arrow Publications #118, 1950, Canadian), $137.

Terror at Night (Avon Books #110, PBO 1947) anthology featuring HPL and other horror authors, $133.

The Girl with the Hungry Eyes, edited by Donald A. Wollheim (Avon Books #184), $115.

Into Plutonian Depths by Stanton Coblentz (Avon Books #281), $110.

An Earthman on Venus by Ralph M. Farley (Avon Books #285), $137.

The Ship of Ishtar by A.A. Merritt (Avon #324), $100.

The Moon Pool by A.A. Merritt (Avon Books #370), $110.

The Green Girl by Jack Williamson (Avon Fantasy Novel #2), $133.

Flesh by Philip Jóse Farmer (Beacon #277, PBO), $121.

Time Trap by Rog Phillips (Century Book #124, PBO), $133.

INSTANT EXPERT

The Black Flame *by Stanley Weinbaum (Harlequin Books #205, 1950s), this Canadian publisher originally published SF and crime novels, not romance!*

Typewriter in the Sky by L. Ron Hubbard (British Cherry Tree #409), scarce, $440.

Doctor Death #2 by Zorro (Corinth #121), $101.

Terror Tales #1 (Corinth #143, anthology), $242.

Terror Tales #2 (Corinth #147, anthology), $302.

It's All in Your Mind by Robert Bloch (Curtis #7156), $110.

The Crimson Witch by Dean Koontz (Curtis #7156, PBO), $110.

Galactic Storm by John Brunner (Curtis-Warren, U.K., PBO), his first book, $187.

Saturn Patrol by E.C. Tubb (Curtis-Warren, U.K., his first book), $110.

Universe by Robert A. Heinlein (Dell 10-Cent #36), $133.

The War of the Worlds by H.G. Wells (Dell Books), $152.

Brigands of the Moon by John W. Campbell (Duchess, Canadian), $190.

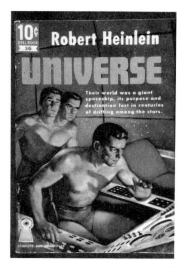

Universe
*by Robert A. Heinlein
(Dell Ten-Cent Books
#36, 1950), with
incredible Robert
Stanley two-headed
mutant cover.*

The Image of the Beast by Philip Jóse Farmer (Essex House #0108, PBO), $132.

A Feast Unknown by Philip Jóse Farmer (Essex House #0121, PBO), $182.

Fear by L. Ron Hubbard (Galaxy Novel #29), $110.

I Am Legend by Richard Matheson (Gold Medal Books #417, PBO), $165.

The Shrinking Man by Richard Matheson (Gold Medal Books #577, PBO), $165.

Those Sexy Saucer People by George H. Smith (Greenleaf #220, PBO, sex and SF), $165.

The House that Stood Still by A.E. van Vogt (Harlequin Books #177, Canadian), $226.

The Black Flame by Stanley Weinbaum (Harlequin Books #205, Canadian), $247.

The Golden Amazon by John Russell Fearn (Harlequin Books #218, Canadian), $330.

The Lost World by Arthur Conan Doyle (Harlequin Books #238, Canadian), $134.

INSTANT EXPERT

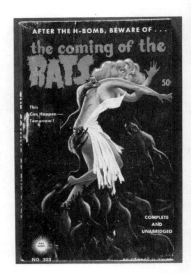

The Coming of the Rats *by George H. Smith (Pike Books #203, PBO, 1960s), classic cover for a novel that mixes SF with soft-core sex.*

The Dying Earth by Jack Vance (Hillman Book #41, 1950), $364.

The Shadow and the Voice of Murder by Maxwell Grant (L.A. Bantam #21): for text cover version, $443.; for illustrated cover version, $1,500.

The Tides of Lust by Samuel R. Delaney (Lancer #71344, PBO 1973, mixes SF with sex), $137.

The Coming of the Rats by George H. Smith (Pike Book #203, PBO), $150.

Pinocchio by C. Collodi (Pocket Books #18), $221.

Dr. Jekyll and Mr. Hyde by R.L. Stevenson (Pocket Books #123), $110.

Pinocchio by C. Collodi (Whitman #556), $875.

The Whispering Gorilla by David K. Reed (World Fantasy Classic #2, British, 1950), $660.

20 COLLECTIBLE SF/F/H/ PUBLISHER IMPRINTS AND SERIES

Over the decades there have been quite a few publisher imprints and book series that have become

COLLECTING SCIENCE FICTION AND FANTASY

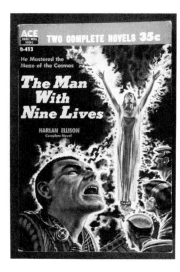

The Man with Nine Lives *by Harlan Ellison, one-half of Ace Double #D-413 (backed with Ellison's* A Touch of Infinity*), cover by Ed Emsh.*

collectible in their own right or of interest to collectors. There are also some of these that have good future collectible potential. Here are some examples:

ACE BOOKS:
Begun in 1952, this publisher, under editor Donald A. Wollheim was heavily influenced by the old pulp magazines, with SF stories full of adventure and action. With Ballantine Books, Ace was one of two specialist science fiction mass-market paperback publishers. Ace published many books, most of which in the "D," "F," and "Ace SF Specials" series are very collectible and are listed below.

ACE DOUBLES:
The original Ace Books that began with Ace Books #D-1 in 1952 and continued with their first SF book Ace Books #D-13, *Cry Plague!* The famous and highly collectible "D" series contains many fine books including PBO's by Philip K. Dick. A very popular series.

ACE SCIENCE FICTION SPECIALS:
Actually three series of paperback originals generally from the 1960s, 70s, and 80s that featured the

INSTANT EXPERT

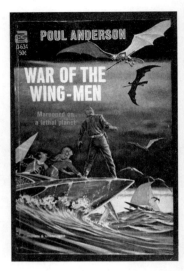

War of the Wing-Men *by Poul Anderson (Ace Books #G-634, 1960s), early Anderson novel and typical 1960s Ace SF novel.*

cream of the crop of Ace authors, and many classic and influential SF novels. Many of these books are very collectible PBO's and will become big money books.

AVON FANTASY READERS:
A digest anthology series from Avon Books that reprinted classic pulp SF/F/H stories (mostly from *Weird Tales*), and the best *WT* authors and work. There are 18 digests in the series containing great GGA and monster cover art very popular with collectors, and were published from 1947 to 1952.

BALLANTINE ADULT FANTASY SERIES:
Published from about 1969 to 1974, usually with the famous unicorn logo, this series of almost a hundred books contained many first paperback printings and reprints of great classic fantasy and horror that had not seen publication in decades. This series, edited by Lin Carter, was a great service to fantasy fans and readers worldwide, and these books were the seed from which today's fantasy boom has grown. A very collectible series that

COLLECTING SCIENCE FICTION AND FANTASY

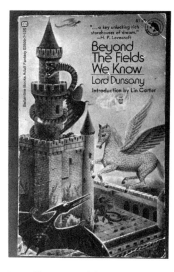

Beyond the Fields We Know *by Lord Dunsany (Ballantine, 1970s), classic fantasy and a fine example of the quality of the Ballantine Adult Fantasy series.*

is still acquirable and capable of being completed by collectors.

BALLANTINE BOOKS:
Founded by Ian and Betty Ballantine in 1952, these innovators published much SF/F/H as original paperbacks and hardcovers that are very much collected. Ballantine Books was one of two publishers (with Ace Books) that became the first science fiction specialist publishers in 1952 and specialized in more serious and adult work. There are many good books, imprints, and series in the Ballantine run, some are listed below.

BALLANTINE HARDCOVER BOOKS:
Published simultaneously with the Ballantine PBO's in the early and middle 1950s, these small books were hardcovers with dustjackets and many are very scarce first editions. They are very collectible and very pricey.

BALLANTINE HORROR SERIES:
A series published in the late 1970s, usually with the devil head logo, featuring many fine horror

INSTANT EXPERT

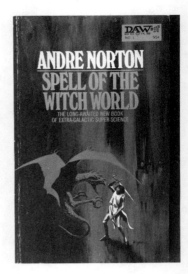

Spell of the Witch World *by Andre Norton (Daw Books #1, PBO, 1972). The first DAW book.*

books. This series contains an especially nice collection of reprints of the works of H.P. Lovecraft. An understated series that deserves more attention and will become collectible in its own right in the future.

BALLANTINE STAR SERIES:
A series of original anthologies and novels (PBO's) published by Ballantine Books from 1953 until the late 1950s. The series was edited by Fred Pohl. This was the first original anthology series and was far ahead of its time. Underrated, but an influential and historically significant SF series of paperbacks.

BEAGLE BOOKS and BOXER BOOKS:
Two early 1970s imprints of Ballantine Books, rather obscure and featuring great horror titles by H.P. Lovecraft as well as some SF by Ron Goulart and others with stunning Vincent DiFate covers. A low-key series but worth the look.

DAW BOOKS:
The DAW stands for Donald A. Wollheim, who in 1972 left Ace Books and began his own imprint at New American Library, Signet Book (NAL). The

series began with DAW Books #1, *Witch World* by Andre Norton, and continued with over a thousand books, mostly PBO's. DAW is still active and has been instrumental in bringing out many fine books and many new authors. All DAW Books have collector numbers and they are poised to be sure-fire future collectibles in the next century.

DAW YEARS BEST HORROR STORIES:
A series of first edition anthologies that collect the best short horror from the 1980s and 1990s. A very influential series and highly collectible because these volumes contain many great small press stories that only appeared in small and obscure magazines.

DELL ABYSS:
The late 1980s and early 1990s horror fiction imprint of Dell Books, with many covers by Harry O. Morris. Many of these are PBO's and worthy of notice by collectors. An imprint that has great future potential.

DEL REY BOOKS:
Originally a SF/F imprint of Ballantine Books begun by Judy Lynn Benjamin Del Rey and then run by her husband, Lester del Rey, after her death. Del Rey was an upscale publisher of SF and fantasy, with the accent more on fantasy. Much excellent material was published in this series and good new books came out all the time.

DOC SAVAGE:
A series of over 100 paperbacks that reprint the adventures of this 30's–40's pulp magazine hero and his crime-fighting crew. The first printings are first editions; later double and triple omnibus volumes are scarce, some Philip Jóse Farmer and Will Murray PBO's also. A very good and collected series. Great covers by Bama and others.

INSTANT EXPERT

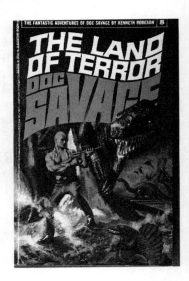

The Land of Terror
*by Kenneth Robeson
(Bantam Books, 1st
ed. 1963), classic pulp
reprint paperback
series with James
Bama cover art.*

LASER BOOKS:
An SF imprint of Harlequin Books (the romance publisher from Canada) which published a series of 56 PBO's from 1975 to 1977, including books by K.W. Jeter, Tim Powers, and a Dean Koontz (*Invasion*) written under the name of Aaron Wolfe. A very collectible series, the last three books were not sold to the public but through subscription so they are scarce and in demand.

PERRY RHODAN:
A series of over 100 SF space opera novels reprinted from the original German by Ace Books with stunning Gray Morrow cover art. A collectible series, but very flat in value at the moment.

PULPHOUSE SHORT STORY PAPERBACKS:
Slim rack-size paperbacks of about 40 to 50 pages published from 1991 to about 1994—actually a SF/F/H series of PBO and first edition novellas and noveletes with about 60 books published in the series. These will become quite collectible in years to come. I also believe that the distribution was

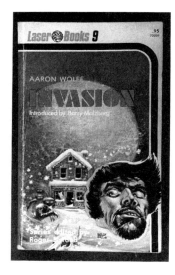

Invasion
*by Aaron Wolfe
(Laser Book #9, 1976),
actually written by
Dean Koontz with cover
art by Kelly Freas.*

spotty on these and the print runs small. So they're good prospects.

QUESTAR BOOKS:
The 1980s SF imprint of Popular Library (itself taken over and absorbed into the Ballantine/Random House conglomerate), which published pulp style and adventure-space opera SF.

ROC:
This imprint of NAL (New American Library, or Signet Books) was an SF imprint that was a bit more pulpy in flavor and without the big authors and better writing in the regular Signet line. ROC nevertheless published some good material, including later PBO's by Glen Cook and others.

TIMESCAPE BOOKS:
The SF imprint of Pocket Books during the 1980s which published many fine books by the better SF writers of the time, most being PBO's. This is a very collectible series and is underrated; it is overdue for notice by collectors and discovery by SF fans.

INSTANT EXPERT

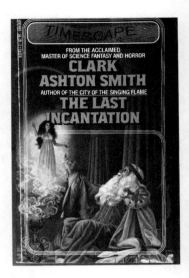

The Last Incantation *by Clark Ashton Smith* (Pocket/Timescape, 1980s), *classic horror with stunning Rowena Morrill cover.*

TOR DOUBLES:

A late 1980s attempt to bring back double paperbacks, a la the old Ace Doubles. There were a few dozen books in the series, and they are very collectible, with some PBO's and other reprints, fine cover art, but not in the pulp tradition. A nice but underappreciated series at the moment.

20 SF/F/H AUTHORS AND THEIR PSEUDONYMS

Many science fiction, fantasy, and horror writers have also written paperbacks outside of these three imaginative genres, and quite often they have written this material under pseudonyms. These can often be found among the Western, general fiction, nonfiction, romance, and especially the soft- and hard-core adult markets. While outside the scope of this book, the reader and collector should realize that a favorite author may have often written books in other genres, and they may be hard to find or unknown because they were published under another name.

There are also quite a few science fiction, fan-

The Rebel of Rhada *by Robert Cham Gilman (Ace Book #71065, PBO, 1960s), SF novel actually written by Alfred Coppel.*

tasy, and horror writers who have used pseudonyms within these fields. Sometimes authors use a different name to differentiate work in one genre from work in another, or sometimes a pseudonym is used for early work, experimental work, or juvenile work within their own genre. Pseudonyms can be used for a variety of reasons. Some authors want to differentiate commercial work from their more serious work. Others may be writing in an area where they are unknown, so sometimes the author (or the publisher or the author's agent) may not want to confuse the public by sending out what might be seen as a mixed message. The use of a pseudonym can also occur because an author wants to hide his true identify. An example of this is the college professor who writes the highly sexual Gor fantasy novels by "John Norman." The reasons for pseudonyms can be endless and endlessly fascinating.

The following list gives a sample of writers in the SF/F/H genres who use pseudonyms in those genres. Also listed is the pseudonym itself, and when known, or surmised, why the pen name may have been used.

INSTANT EXPERT

Asimov, Isaac: as Paul French, his "Lucky Starr" series of juvenile SF adventures were published under this pen name.

Brunner, John: as Keith Woodcott for a couple of PBO SF novels that he wrote for Ace Books in the 1960s. Good adventure SF but not his usual serious work.

Coppel, Alfred: as Robert Cham Gilman, one book for Ace Books, a fantasy from the 1960s called *The Rebel of Rhada*, Coppel has written many fine books.

Fearn, John Russell: as Vargo Statten and the later books of Volstead Gribdan in British PBO SF digests in the 1950s. Very collectible books.

King, Stephen: as Richard Bachman, four PBO horror novels published by Signet in the early 1980s, very collectible and done to prove King's quality of work. The books became hits and many unknowing reviewers of the time proclaimed Bachman as the new Stephen King!

Koontz, Dean: as Leigh Nichols, horror and gothic novels marketed as romance in the late 1970s and early 1980s. Now being reprinted under Koontz's name.

Kornbluth, C.M.: as Jordan Park for non-SF novels in the 1950s from Lion Books; as Cyril Judd (with Judith Merril) for *Sin in Space* (Beacon SF novel), *Gunner Cade* (Ace Books), and others.

Kuttner, Henry: as Lewis Padgett with his wife C.L. Moore, some SF and F novels and collections.

Malzbery, Barry: as K.M. O'Donnell, for some of his books for Ace; less serious work.

Moorcock, Michael: as Edward P. Bradbury for a trilogy of Edgar Rice Burroughs pastiche novels published in the U.K. by Compact Books in the 1960s and reprinted in the U.S. by Lancer Books in the early 1970s. *Blades of Mars*, etc., also other names.

Moore, C.L.: as Lewis Padgett with her husband Henry Kuttner.

Nelson, Ray: as Jeffery Lord, Nelson wrote one book in the Blade series by Lord as a work-for-hire.

Norton, Andre: actually Mary Alice Norton whose first Ace book was published under the name Andrew North. Norton then took the Andre Norton pseudonym and has been Andre Norton ever since. She is known by this name today.

Offutt, Andrew: as John Cleve for a series of light sex and SF paperbacks from the 1970s.

Silverberg, Robert: as Robert Randall with Randall Garrett for some books; also as Ivar P. Jorgenson for some other books. Probably many more.

Tubb, E.C.: as King Lang, his first novel *Saturn Patrol*, and later many books as Volstead Gridban in the U.K.

Turtledove, Harry: as Eric Iverson, two Viking novels and PBO's published by Belmont Books in the late 1970s before Turtledove became a hit SF author.

Westlake, Donald: as Curt Clarke, one book for Ace, a PBO in 1966, *Anarchaos*, from this primarily crime fiction author.

Wollheim, Donald A.: as David Grinnell, for a couple of PBO SF novels published by Ace Books when he was editor there. Obviously to deflect criticism of him publishing his own books. They're not bad books, either.

Collector's Guide

REFERENCE MATERIAL

The successful collector uses many resources to aid him or her in discovering what books are worthwhile reading, which books to collect, and which books are worth money. The following references will aid you by offering a fountain of valuable information. While there are literally hundreds of books written on these topics, I feel the ones below offer the best information on a diversity of topics and are more easily available.

Magazines:

I have listed only magazines currently published and still available.

Paperback Parade: The Magazine for Paperback Readers and Collectors, is the longest-running magazine in the hobby. I have proudly been publishing it since 1986 with 46 issues having appeared so far. It is geared 100 percent to the pb collector, and covers all aspects and genres of collectible paperbacks. It features detailed articles and interviews with collectible writers and artists, as well as material on scarce books and publisher series with many cover art photos. Published bi-monthly, it runs 100-plus pages with color covers, digest size, and costs $7 per issue. Subscriptions in the U.S. third class mail are six issues for $35. Outside the U.S. six/$42. Available from Gryphon Publications, PO Box 209, Brooklyn, NY 11228-0209 USA.

Paperback, Pulp and Comic Collector: A fine British magazine in book form, 140 pages and with color covers. The main focus here is U.K. and U.S. collectible paperbacks but there is also material on comics and pulp magazines. Available from Gryphon Publications (see address above) in the U.S. for $10 per copy; or from the publisher: Zardoz Books, 20 Whitecroft, Dilton Marsh, Westbury, Wilts., England, for about 7 Pounds, or $12. So far three issues have been published.

The Fantastic Collector: A fanzine that has articles and material on the old pulps, hardcover and paperback books, and classic and collectible SF/F/H authors, especially Edgar Rice Burroughs. A six-issue bi-monthly sub is $24 first class from: Camille Cazedessus, PO Box 2340, Pagosa Springs, CO 81147, USA.

Locus: one of two fine SF/F trade magazines, loaded with articles and material on SF and new books. Available from Locus Publications, PO Box 13305, Oakland, CA 94681.

SF Chronicle: The other fine SF/F trade magazine is full of articles and reviews and much SF material and new books. Available from: Andrew Porter, PO Box 2730, Brooklyn, NY 11201-2730, USA.

Books:
British Science Fiction Paperbacks and Magazines 1949–1956, an annotated bibliography and guide by Philip Harbottle and Stephen Holland (Borgo Press, PBO 1994), lists hundreds of collectible 1950s British SF digests with capsule descriptions of the story of each. A companion volume to the same authors' earlier, *Vultures of the Void* (see

below). A fine and extensive work with much new valuable information.

Danse Macabre by Stephen King (First Edition: Everest House hardcover from 1981; first mass-market paperback: Berkley Books #06462X, 1983; many reprints). King's only nonfiction book, an examination and study of the history of horror fiction with his own personal comments and reminiscences. An interesting book for King fans, but also a fine overview of the horror field with keen insight into horror paperback publishing. A key reference book and very underrated.

Hancer's Price Guide to Paperback Books by Kevin Hancer (Wallace-Homestead Books, 3rd edition, 1990, $16.95), the latest edition of this price guide. The book is an excellent listing of vintage paperbacks by publisher, but take the prices with a grain of salt.

Hawk's Authors' Pseudonyms II by Pat Hawk (self-published, 2nd edition, 1995), a massive large-size hardcover of 400 pages with almost every author listed who has used a pseudonym and that pseudonym. Introduction by Joe Lansdale. An essential for any library or serious collector, it sells for about $60 but write to the author/publisher for info at: 1740 Sunshine Lane, Southlake, TX 76092-9543, USA.

Official Price Guide to Paperbacks by Jon Warren (House of Collectibles, PBO 1991), probably the best price guide with extensive listings, though you should take the prices here with a grain of salt. A new edition is due in 1997. An essential book for its bibliographic information, but not the prices.

Over My Dead Body by Lee Server (Chronicle Books, 1994, PBO, $16.95), an excellent overview of the collectible paperback field and loaded with many wonderful color cover reproductions of the most important and collectible books.

Paperbacks at Auction by Joe Crifo and John Gargiso (Gorgon Books, PBO 1995, $20), a fat book full of all paperback auction results (over 16,000 entries), from 1991 to 1994. Essential information for any bookseller or collector. Available from Gryphon Publications for $20 (see address above); or from the publisher Gorgon Books (see address on specialized dealers page).

Paperbacks USA by Piet Schreuders (Blue Dolphin Books, 1981, $10.95), probably the best book ever published about paperback cover art and the artists who did the vintage covers. A wonderful excursion into the topic with many photos. While it is out of print, copies turn up from time to time (usually in the collectible market for $20 to $25), and it is an excellent book in all respects. Essential reading.

The Movie Tie-in Book by Moe Wadle (Nostalgia Books #1, PBO 1994), a fine book on movie tie-in paperbacks of all kinds, and also lists paperback tie-ins for SF/F/H films. Available for $15 from Gryphon Publications (see the address above); or from the publisher: Nostalgia Books, 1410 10th Street, Coralville, IA 52241-1718, USA.

Vultures of the Void by Philip Harbottle and Stephen Holland (Borgo Press, PBO 1992), an extensive and detailed study of postwar British science fiction and fantasy publishing. A fascinating read and loaded with valuable new information. A companion volume was written by the same authors and published later as *British Science Fiction Paperbacks and Magazines 1949–1956*, also worthwhile. You can order these both for $20 each from Gryphon Publications (see address above); or from the publisher: Borgo Press, PO Box 2845, San Bernardino, CA 92406, USA.

DIRECTORY OF SPECIALIZED PAPERBACK DEALERS

Here's where you can buy the books you have seen and read about in this book. Send a SASE for info and the latest list put out by these dealers. And let them know you heard about them from this book.

All the following dealers are mail-order dealers with various types of catalogs. In addition, some also have stores you can visit (marked with an *), and some accept want lists (marked thus, **).

BLACK ACE BOOKS: 1658 Griffith Park Blvd., Los Angeles, CA 90026, vintage paperback dealer, also auctions, *, **

BLACK HILL BOOKS: The Wain House, Black Hill, Clunton, Craven Arms, Shropshire, SY7-0DJ, England, run by U.K. horror author Guy N. Smith and his wife, Jean, with a good selection of all U.K. and U.S. genres, especially horror. **

MARTIN BLANK: 220 St. Mary's Road, Winnipeg, Manitoba, R2H-1JB, Canada, a new dealer just starting out and who should be in action in 1997, **

NICK CERTO: PO Box 10305, Newburgh, NY 12552, carries recent and new books of all kinds, especially SF/F/H, ** on newer items, also some vintage.

DIMESTORE BOOKS: Royce Allen, 4255 S. Buckley Rd. #169, Aurora, CO 80013, vintage paperback dealer, **

CHRIS DRUMM BOOKS: PO Box 445, Polk City, IA 50226, lists only new material and much small press and obscure items, lots of stock, ** for newer material.

GORGON BOOKS: 102 JoAnne Drive, Holbrook, NY 11741, vintage paperback dealers, also hardcovers and auctions. They also publish *Paperbacks at Auction*.

KAYO BOOKS: Ron Blum, 814 Post St., San Francisco, CA 94109, vintage paperback dealer, *, **

KIDS, CRIME AND CHAOS: Steve Brown, PO Box 148, Northolt, Middlesex, VB5-5TR, England, vintage SF/F/H and more in U.S. and U.K. editions, auctions, also **

HENRI LABELLE: 1162 Lesage St., PO Box 561, Prevost, Quebec, JOR-1TO, Canada, good selection of U.S. and foreign pbs of all kinds, also auctions.

MICHEL LANTEIGNE: 5468 St. Urbain #4, Montreal, Quebec, Canada, vintage paperback dealer, good selection of Canadian, foreign, and U.S. pbs, also auctions, **

MCGEENEY'S BOOKS: 1315 South Mason, Tacoma, WA 98405, vintage paperback dealer, *, **

MODERN AGE BOOKS: Jeff Canja, PO Box 325, East Lansing, MI 48826, vintage paperback dealer, auctions, **, a good assortment.

WAYNE MULLINS: 2337 Marshell Rd., Wetumpka, AL 36092, vintage paperback dealer, **

LYNN MUNROE BOOKS: PO Box 1736, Orange, CA 92668, vintage paperback dealer, also auctions, **

TIM MURPHY: 31 Hewlett Rd., Red Hook, NY 12571, vintage paperback dealer, **

OLD PUEBLO BOOKS: PO Box 17898, Tucson, AZ 85731, vintage and newer paperback dealer, *, **

PANDORA'S BOOKS: PO Box 54, Neche, ND 58265, massive magazine-size list of all paperbacks in all genres, **

WALLY PATTENGILL: Route 3, Box 508, Waco, TX 76708, vintage paperbacks of all types.

JEFF PATTON: 3621 Carolina St. NW, Massillon, OH 44646, vintage paperback dealer, **

BUD PLANT: PO Box 1689, Grass Valley, CA 95945, his catalog has a lot of SF/F/H paperbacks, hardcovers, comics, art, etc.

RIVER OAKS BOOKS: RFD 2 - Box 5505, Jay, ME 04239, vintage paperback dealer and auctions, **

NORMAN TANQUAY: 1136 Pelican Pl., Safety Harbor, FL 34695, vintage paperback dealer

PHIL THOMAS: 2790 Washington Blvd., Arlington, VA 22201, vintage paperback dealer, strong in SF/F/H and Ace Doubles, etc.

G. WARLOCK VANCE: 12809 Astor Ave., Cleveland, OH 44135, vintage paperback dealer but very heavy into horror.

ROBERT AND PHYLISS WEINBERG: 15145 Oxford Drive, Oak Forest, IL 60452, have a big catalog of new and recent books of all kinds but specialize in SF/F/H, ** on newer books, and issue a vintage paperback catalog also.

IAN VANCE: 1560 Superior Ave. #A3, Costa Mesa, CA 92627, vintage paperback dealer.

BOB WARDZINSKI: 12 Rosamund Ave., Merley, Wimborne, Dorset, BH21-1TE, England, vintage paperback dealer, many U.K. editions, **

JON WHITE: 98 Riverside Drive, New York, NY 10024, specialist paperback dealer, no lists but will work from want list. Expert in SF/F/H.

ZARDOZ BOOKS: 20 Whitecroft, Dilton Marsh, Westbury, Wilts., England, massive listings of all genres of U.S. and U.K. paperbacks and pulps, puts out London PB show each year and publishers *Paperback*, *Pulp and Comic Collector* magazine, **

PAPERBACK SHOWS AND CONVENTIONS

There are several annual specialty paperback collector shows as well as other conventions (usually SF/F/H) that have dealers in out-of-print and rare books. These are all good places to find books and sometimes incredible bargains can be found at these events. They're also a lot of fun to attend and just seeing all those wonderful old books in one room is a joy to behold.

INSTANT EXPERT

Specialty Collectible Paperback Shows

THE NEW YORK COLLECTIBLE PAPERBACK EXPO: In its ninth year, it's held each September in the NYC area. This is my own show and has dozens of specialty paperback dealers from all over the country, fans and collectors from all over the U.S., Canada, and the U.K., and many special authors and artists attend. Some of the hot or collectible authors of today and tomorrow are at these shows today. For information on the 1997 show, or to reserve selling space, contact me through Paperback Parade/Gryphon Publications, PO Box 209, Brooklyn, NY 11228-0209, USA.

PAPERBACK COLLECTORS' SHOW AND SALE: A great big show held once a year in March in Los Angeles, with many books and guests. All dealers are specialty paperback dealers. The New York and L.A. shows are the two big U.S. shows and neither should be missed. For information contact Tom Lesser (818) 349-3844 or Rose at Black Ace Books (213) 661-5052.

PORTLAND PAPERBACK BOOK PARTY: A three-day book festival in Portland, Oregon, held each August. It's the longest-running paperback show, the 1996 show being the twentieth annual event. Many books and guests and much good talk and comradeship. Contact Lance Casebeer (503) 641-7523 for information.

BRITISH PAPERBACK SHOW: Held each year in London, England, a fine U.K. version of the U.S. shows. A great reason to visit London, held annually since 1991. Many U.S. and U.K. books and many guests. Contact Maurice Flanagan, Zardoz Books, 20 Whitecroft, Dilton Marsh, Westbury, Wilts., England.

Other Shows: Following are various shows and conventions (cons) that have good dealer rooms and are worth attending to find collectible books. These are usually held in different cities and put on by different groups of people (or committees) each year.

PULPCON: One of the best shows, devoted to the collecting of the old pulp magazines, held once a year, and always worth going to. Many good paperback and book deals can be found here and prices are good.

BOUCHERCON: The annual mystery convention held in a different city each year. While not related to SF/F/H, it is a good place to pick up books, and you'll often be surprised what you may find in the dealer room there.

WORLD SCIENCE FICTION CONVENTION: Held each year during the Labor Day weekend, a massive four- to five-day affair, a SF/F/H extravaganza, and a huge dealer room that is partially book related. Definitely worth a visit and worth the experience.

ATLANTA FANTASY FAIR: A big convention held each year in Atlanta, mostly for fantasy and horror, and a good place to buy books and meet many of the newer authors.

SAN DIEGO COMICS CON: a massive con held each year in San Diego, related specifically to comic books but always interesting, and the odd items do turn up. You might be surprised and it is fun.

PAPERBACK AUCTIONS AND AUCTION HOUSES

Auction houses offer the serious collector a unique chance to obtain rare, scarce, and other often hard-to-find books. Many books appear at auction that even some long-time collectors have never seen before. Auctions do the collector a great service but it must be remembered that their sole reason for existence is to get the highest possible price for each book sold.

INSTANT EXPERT

When you bid and buy from an auction house you must realize that you (and your dollars) are in competition with every collector who bids on that particular book. Since auctions usually contain only a single copy of each type of book, you can see that all it can take to make the price escalate is just two people who want that book badly enough. These are often very scarce books in prime condition, and they are in great demand by collectors. They can sometimes go for a mighty price. It is not uncommon for people at auctions to pay far in excess of the actual value a book may be worth (after all, it is easy to get caught up in the bidding frenzy) or sometimes overpay for an edition they may later realize they did not really want. On the other hand, they may just decide it's worth paying big money for an edition they simply cannot live without. There are also real bargains to be had at auctions: for instance, if you are the only bidder on a particular book, you can get many fine and key books for a very modest price. Auctions and the bidding action are also a lot of fun. Prices realized, however, can also lend an inflated value to many of the books. This is because it can take only two overzealous collectors to drive up the price realized on a book to unrealistic heights. Remember, just because a book received a high bid does not mean it is worth that price in the market. It's only worth that price to the person who bought the book. So proper care should be taken when participating in auctions.

Auctions are also great fun and an opportunity to get the scarce books that you've never seen or that just don't seem to turn up any more. All of the auction houses I have listed here are highly recommended, their honesty and integrity have been tested over the years, and the people from the auction houses are knowledgeable book lovers and fans. They're nice, fun people to deal with. Many of these auction houses send out attractive catalogs, with photos (some in color) of all of the actual books that you can bid on. These catalogs are often expensive to produce, but you're not required to buy something in each auction to keep getting them. However, you do have to show an interest, and if after a certain number of auctions you do not participate, you may be asked to subscribe or be dropped from the catalog list. To help defray the cost of the catalogs, some auction houses charge $5 or $10 as a subscription.

Specialty Paperback Auction Houses: See their listing in the previous section for addresses.

BLACK ACE BOOKS

GORGON BOOKS

COLLECTING PAPERBACKS?: Lance Casebeer: Lance only does auctions and the Portland Book Party; see his address in the show section in previous pages.

KIDS, CRIME, AD CHAOS (U.K.)

HENRI LABELLE (Canada)

MICHEL LANTEIGNE (Canada)

MODERN AGE BOOKS

LYNN MUNROE BOOKS

RIVER OAKS BOOKS

How to Sell Your Collection

Since this book has showed you how to collect, how to buy, and what to buy, we'll now take a look at the other end of the hobby. When you have a collection to sell, you can basically do one of two things. Sell the collection outright to a dealer as a lot (or if it's a large collection with key material, to a group of dealers in a few choice lots), or become a dealer yourself. Both of these methods have their own advantages and disadvantages. We'll take a brief look at them now.

Becoming a Dealer

If you have a large collection of quality and key books in nice shape, this is probably the best way to realize the most profit from your collection. However, there is a lot of work involved. You must have the time to conduct a business. This means attending some shows, designing, placing, and paying for ads, and individually grading and pricing each and every book at a price at which it will sell. You will need to compile a catalog or sales list, not an easy task. Many collector-dealers or collectors who sell their collection as dealers have to be careful that all the good books are not gobbled up too early by being underpriced, thus leaving you holding the bag with a lot of lesser condition and non-key, low-demand items. This can happen if you're not careful.

The advantages of selling your books yourself are the obvious ones: You have the possibility of gaining the maximum retail price for the books (more than any dealer would ever pay you). You can realize a very nice profit and you can also have a lot of fun selling books. It's a business, but it's also a wonderful and exciting activity for a book lover. And you can make money if you do it right.

The people you'll meet and the deals you'll run across and make may even give you the bug to continue even after most of your initial selling stock from your own collection has been sold. You'll know soon enough if book dealing is right for you, if you enjoy it, and if you can turn a profit.

Selling to a Dealer

Of course, it goes without saying that you'll get a lot less when you sell to a dealer. Dealers like to buy large lots and usually offer flat fees based on the number of books or will pay a flat rate of one, two, or three dollars per book. They want the key books in near Fine condition (or at least strict VG), and may offer prices on individual copies if your books are the better items.

Naturally it's always best to shop around when selling to dealers. Get offers, counter offers, and offers from various dealers. The paperback dealers listed in this book are all highly recommended, and since they are all paperback specialists, they will offer you their best price possible for your books. Just don't jump at the first offer, and realize that even if you want to sell your books quickly, even selling outright to a dealer (and you want to be sure to sell to the *right* dealer), it may take some time. In any event, it will be a lot quicker than if you become a dealer and sell the books yourself. It will also eliminate the extra work and expense of being a dealer if you wholesale your entire collection to a paperback dealer.

When you are selling your collection, you really have to see what works best for you. What do you want from the sale? Quick cash? A good return on investment? To get rid of it quickly? Will you take a loss? What time frame do you have? How much time do you have to sell it? All these considerations should be carefully examined before you decide to sell anything, so you can draw up a reasonable and successful plan of operation that will enable you to realize the maximum return when you sell your books.

INSTANT EXPERT QUIZ

1. What should be the minimum condition acceptable for a collectible vintage paperback?

2. Name the author who almost singlehandedly created the 1980's horror boom.

3. What was the price realized at auction for a copy of *The Shadow and the Voice of Murder* (L.A. Bantam # 21) with illustrated cover?

4. What was the first paperback to use the term "science fiction"?

5. What does PBO mean?

6. Name the husband and wife artist team whose serious and adult-surreal art graces many collectible science fiction paperbacks.

7. Name the author who created Conan the Barbarian.

8. What year did Ace Books and Ballantine Books begin publishing?

9. The classic horror novel *The Werewolf of Paris* by Guy Endore had three early vintage editions. Who were the publishers?

10. What was Jack Vance's first book?

INSTANT EXPERT

11. Name the two SF novels made into popular counterculture films in the 1960s?

12. What was the film that began the 1970s SF boom?

13. Name the new six-part serial novel by Stephen King that has already become collectible.

14. ARC stands for what term?

15. This short-run series of vintage paperbacks has almost every book as scarce or rare.

16. Finish the phrase: "Best condition is …"

17. What recent publisher imitated the old Ace Doubles with their own collectible SF series?

18. What was the logo for the Ballantine Adult Fantasy series?

19. What famous SF author wrote young adult SF novels under pseudonym Paul French?

20. How many specialty paperback shows are there?

Answers

1. *VG or Very Good*
2. *Stephen King*
3. *$1,500.*
4. The Pocket Book of Science Fiction *(Pocket Books #214, 1943)*
5. *Paperback original, the first time that book has seen print and always a true first edition.*
6. *Leo and Diane Dillon*
7. *Robert E. Howard*
8. *1952*
9. *Pocket Book #97,1941; Avon Book #354, 1951; and Studio Pocket #105 1952 (Canada).*
10. The Dying Earth, *Hillman Book #41 , 1950*
11. A Clockwork Orange *by Anthony Burgess and* Wild in the Streets *by Robert Thom.*

12. Star Wars
13. The Green Mile
14. *Advance reading copy*
15. *L.A. Bantams*
16. *"...always best!"*
17. *Tor Doubles*
18. *Unicorn head*
19. *Isaac Asimov*
20. *4*

ABOUT THE AUTHOR

GARY LOVISI is the founder of Gryphon Publications, a small press operating in Brooklyn, New York. He is also the publisher and editor of *Paperback Parade*, a bi-monthly magazine devoted to rare and collectible paperbacks, paperback publishing history, and the authors and artists of the books. Lovisi is also the publisher and editor of *Hardboiled* magazine, a showcase for the best and hardest cutting-edge crime and suspense fiction appearing today. Recent issues have included work by such greats as Andrew Vachss, Eugene Izzi, Harlan Ellison, Mickey Spillane, Joe Lansdale, Richard Lupoff, William F. Nolan, Lawrence Block, and other fine writers.

Lovisi's nonfiction has appeared in numerous book-related and collector magazines, such as *The Armchair Detective*, *Bookcase*, *Romantic Times*, *Strange New Worlds Science Fiction Collectors Magazine*, and in media/pop-culture magazines such as *Baby Boomer Collectibles* and *Cool Stuff*. He has an ongoing book column in *The Fantastic Collector*, which is also reprinted in Europe in the Belgian magazine *Horizon*. Scholarly articles by Lovisi on such topics as paperback books and talk shows will appear in the forthcoming *History of the Mass Media in the United States: an Encyclopedia* (Garland Books, New York, 1997).

His books *on* books, focus on collector and bibliographic information. *Science Fiction Detective Tales* (PBO 1986; to be reprinted in an updated and expanded edition in 1997) is a look at futuristic detective fiction in paperback; *Dashiell Hammett and Raymond Chandler* (PBO 1994) is a bibliography of the various paperback appearances of these two famous hardboiled authors. *Sherlock Holmes: the Great Detective in Paperback* (1991; a new, expanded edition is scheduled for 1997) focuses on all the Holmes material by Doyle *and* others appearing in paperback in the U.S. and the U.K.

Lovisi is the founder and sponsor of the New York Collectible Paperback Expo, an annual booklovers convention now in its 9th year that features dealers from all over the U.S. and many famous authors and artists.

A collector himself, for over 25 years, Lovisi is often called upon to write material on or about books and book collecting.

Lovisi's most recent works are fiction: a hardboiled police procedural, his first Griff and Fats novel, *Hellbent on Homicide* (Scarlet Press, PBO 1995), and a short story crime collection, *Extreme Measures: 15 Stories of Murder, Mayhem, Mystery and Madness* (Gryphon Books, PBO 1996). These books will be reprinted in the U.K. in 1997.

INDEX

Ace Books, 23, 24, 37, 42, 44, 94, 105, 107
Anderson, Poul, 53, 78, *106*
Armed Service Editions (ASE's), 25–26, 27, 31, 38
Asimov, Isaac, 10–11, 53, 114
auctions, 10–17, 20, 97–104, 125–27
Avon Books, 28, 29, 31–34, 36, 39–40, 43, 106

Ballantine Books, 24, 37, 42, 44, 60–61, 78–79, 94, 105, 106, 107, 108
Bantam Books, 47, 58, 60, 94
Bloch, Robert, 11, 23, 44, 51, 55, *65*, 99, 102
books on collectibles, 118–20
Bradbury, Ray, 29, 47, *80*
Bradley, Marion Zimmer, 11, 57, 78
Brunner, John, 53, 102, 114
budgeting collection, 17–20, 73
Burroughs, Edgar Rice, 11, 31, 51, 100
buying techniques, 85–90
    dealer's lists, 89–90
    networking, 86–87

cover art, 1–9, 33, 39–41, 42, 43, 46, 48
    collectible artists of, 4–9
Cyberpunk movement, 52, 57

dealers, 19, 74, 75, 89–90, 120–23, 128–29
    lists, 89–90

selling to, 128–29
    specialized paperback, 120–23
Dell Books, 40–41, 47, 109
Dick, Philip K., 11–12, 51, 78, 99, 105
Dunsany, Lord, 28, 31, 79, *107*

Ellison, Harlan, 12, *13*, 80

fantasy. *See under* paperbacks
Farley, Ralph M., 40, *99*, 101
Farmer, Philip Jóse, 101, 103, 109
foreign editions, 90–91
Frank, Pat, 31, 48–49
glossary, 80–84
Gold Medal Books, 45, 76, 77, 88–89
Goulart, Ron, 80, 108
grades of paperbacks, 69–76, 86

hardcovers, 60
Heinlein, Robert A., 12–13, 41, 51, 53, 102
Herbert, Frank, 51, 53
horror. *See under* paperbacks
Howard, Robert E., 13–14, 23, 51, 57, 78, *98*, 99

Jeter, K.W., *15*, 16, 110

King, Stephen, 14–15, 23, 53–55, 79, 114
Koontz, Dean, 15, 55, 79, 102, 110, 114

135

Lansdale, Joe R., *13*, 16, 79, 80
Lovecraft, H.P., 11, *14*, 16, 23, 26, 28, 29, 51, 53, 78, 108
Lowther, George, 38, 100

magazines, 95, 117–18
market trends, 76–80
Matheson, Richard, *15*, 16, 44, 46, 51, 55, 76–77, 79, 80, 103
Merritt, A., 31–32, 33, 39, 43, 100, 101
Moorcock, Michael, 16, 114–15

Norton, Andre, 16, 109, 115

paperbacks
  auction value, 97–104
  collecting, history of, 93–95
  condition of, 69–73, 86
  fantasy, 23, 29–43, 56–58
  grading of, 74–76
  horror, 24–29, 53–56
  movie and TV tie-ins, 49–50, 62–67
  from 1939–1965, 21–43, 71, 95
  from 1952–1970, 44–51
  from 1970s on, 71
  originals (PBO's), 42, 45, 60, 61, 76, 78, 89, 109
  science fiction, 37–43, 52–53
Phillips, Rog, 41–42, *100*, 101
Pocket Books, 21, 28, 29–31, 47, 59, 60, 94, 111
Pohl, Fred, 42, *46*, 108
Powers, Richard, 28–29, 44
pseudonyms of SF/F/H authors, 112–15

publishers of SF/F/H, 23, 26–27, 29, 30–31, 34, 41–42, 44, 47, 104–12. *See also* individual names
  collectible imprints and series, 104–12

Quick Reader Books, 27–28

reference materials, 117–20
reprints, identifying, 87–89

science fiction. *See under* paperbacks
selling, 73, 127–29
  to a dealer, 128–29
shows, 19–20, 89, 123–25
Silverberg, Robert, 78, 115
Smith, Clark Ashton, 23, 51, 79, *112*
Smith, Thorne, 29, 30, 31, 33
Stanley, Robert, 38, 40, 43
Star Trek, 19, 57–60, 61–62, 65, 78
Star Wars, 52, 57–62, 64–65, 78
Stoker, Bram, 22, 28, 53

Tolkien, J.R.R., 23, *24*, 51, 57, 78
trading collectibles, 18

Vance, Jack, 36, 94, 104

want list, 84–85
Wells, H.G., 29, 38, 40, *64*, 102
Williamson, Jack, 40, *42*, 43, 101
Wollheim, Donald A., 22, 34, 37, 38, 39, 101, 105, 108, 115
women authors, collectible, 78